Our American Century

★

Events That Shaped the Century

By the Editors of Time-Life Books, Alexandria, Virginia

With a Foreword by Buzz Aldrin

Contents

★

Foreword

Among the events that have helped shape this century, the ones that have to do with getting off the ground have a very special meaning for me. I made my first airplane flight about 30 years after the Wright brothers made theirs. I was a couple of years old, and my father was flying the single-engine Lockheed Vega painted like an eagle. He was a pioneer in early aviation and a student of Robert Goddard, the father of American rocket research. In those days people ridiculed Goddard because he talked about men going to the Moon some day. That first flight made me sick, but it didn't stop me from wanting to be a pilot. I was a pole-vaulter at West Point and flew jet fighters during the Korean War. Later, for my doctorate at MIT, I wrote my thesis on manned orbital rendezvous. The timing was just right. Some of my concepts were utilized in the Gemini and Apollo flights—and so was I.

I can still recall the strangeness I felt when Neil Armstrong and I landed on the Moon in 1969. There we were, so far away from Earth and yet being watched by so many people back there. To most of them it didn't really make much difference what the rocks we brought back were like. Our journey touched humanity emotionally, and it gave Americans something positive at a time of national turmoil.

But I think the journey's most important aspect was the commitment it represented. We set a goal, and we followed through. I feel sure that Soviet leaders had this demonstration of American resolve in mind when President Reagan threatened to move ahead with his Star Wars defense initiative. Knowing that they couldn't compete with us in another space race, they changed direction, and the Cold War came to an end.

Now I want to see the nation set new goals—developing space tourism, returning to the Moon by 2010, and traveling to Mars by 2020. These are commitments worthy of a new millennium.

*Mounted policemen try to keep traffic moving through
a teeming intersection in downtown Chicago in 1909.*

A bad guy draws a bead on 1920s screen idol Tom Mix. Westerns replete with gunfights, train robberies, horseback chases, and the triumph of good over evil became Hollywood staples in the early part of the century.

1920s airshow daredevils Gladys Roy (right) and Ivan Unger play a pantomime tennis game at 70 miles per hour. The cables holding them to the wings weren't visible to spectators watching nervously from 3,000 feet below.

A migrant worker cradles his baby outside a shanty in California's Imperial Valley in 1937. Farm families driven from the Plains States by prolonged drought swelled the ranks of West Coast migrant workers.

Women workers polish nose cones for A-20 attack bombers at an aviation plant in Long Beach, California. During World War II more than three million women were recruited for war-related jobs.

On August 6, 1946, unmanned naval vessels are dwarfed by a cloud of gas bursting from the ocean a split second after an atomic bomb explodes underwater at Bikini Atoll, the U.S. test site in the Marshall Islands.

Joe DiMaggio hits a double in the 1949 All-Star game. The slugger became a hero in 1941 with an awesome streak of hits in 56 straight games that gave Americans something to cheer about amid gathering war clouds.

A man braces himself as police dogs attack during a civil rights protest in Birmingham, Alabama, in May 1963.

At a hilltop first-aid station in Vietnam, a marine injured in a 1966 firefight reaches out to his buddy. The war claimed 33,000 American casualties that year.

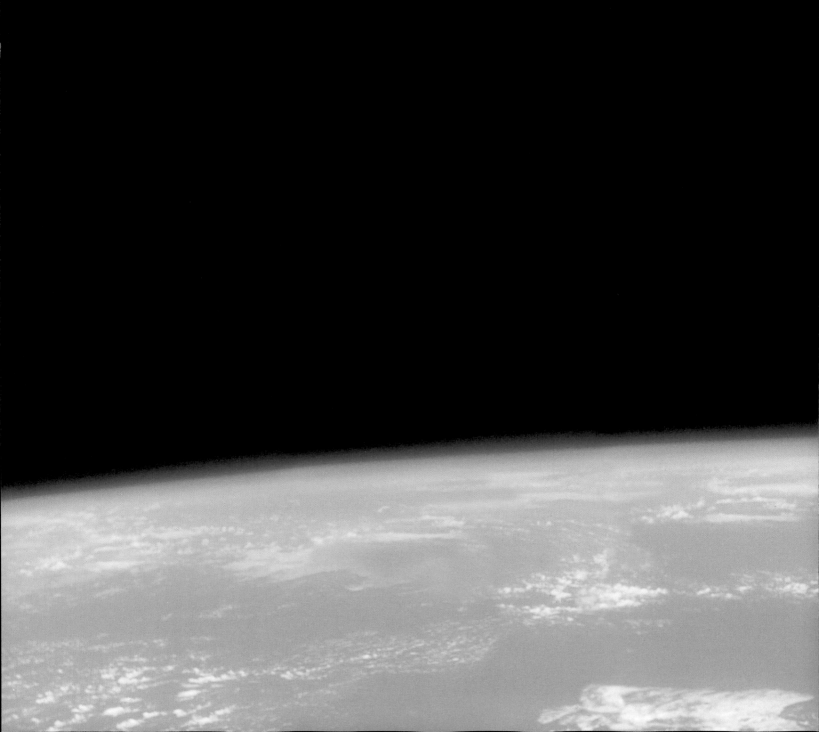

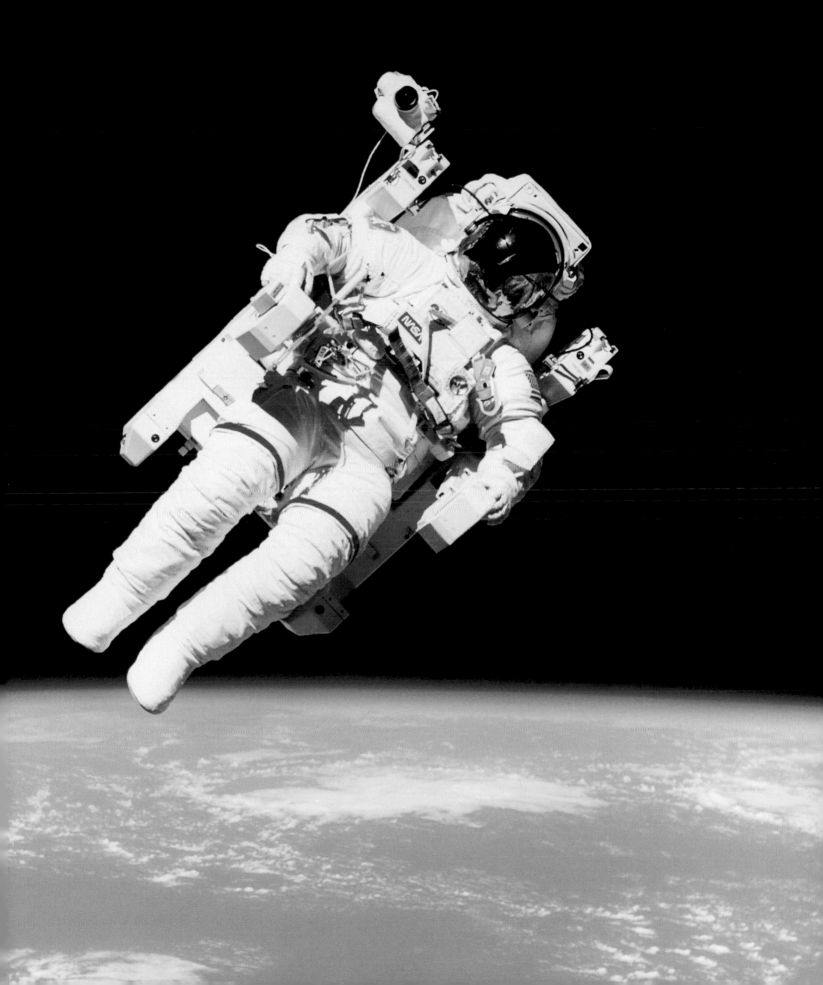

A Nation Transformed: 1900-2000

He never quite looked the part. Rather plump in build, he wore a toothy smile that protruded from beneath a walrus mustache, and he peered at the world with nearsighted difficulty through thick steel-rimmed spectacles. But Theodore Roosevelt needed none of the matinee-idol good looks that would create enthusiastic followings among later generations of political leaders. He possessed such palpable force of presence that he came to symbolize the raw energy of the United States at the turn of the century. The great inventor Thomas Edison thought him "the most striking figure in American life."

Brimming with self-confidence and optimism, Roosevelt embodied the can-do spirit of a nation bursting forth into the 20th century. At every turn he expressed his faith in the inevitability of progress as a nation and as individuals. After all, through force of will, this son of a New York patrician had built himself into vigorous health from a frail boyhood plagued by asthma. Pursuing his "doctrine of the strenuous life, the life of toil and effort," Roosevelt learned to box and then roped cattle and hunted buffalo on his

A forceful Theodore Roosevelt drives a point home during a campaign speech (above). A contemporary said of his energetic delivery, "His teeth snap shut between the syllables, biting them apart."

ranch in the Dakota Territory. During the Spanish-American War, he left his post as assistant secretary of the navy to organize a volunteer regiment of cavalry, the Rough Riders, which he led up San Juan Hill in Cuba. After his triumphant return he was elected governor of New York, then vice president of the United States in 1900. The following year, William McKinley was assassinated, and Roosevelt became at the age of 42 the nation's youngest president ever.

"That damned cowboy," as a political boss in his own Republican Party dubbed him, proceeded to wield the powers of the presidency as no one had before him. He had a motto that summed up his philosophy: "Speak softly and carry a big stick. You will go far." He attacked the business trusts and monopolies—those "malefactors of great wealth." He employed big-stick diplomacy to help Panama win its independence from Colombia so he could start building the Panama Canal. He helped settle the Russo-Japanese War and then sent the Great White Fleet's 16 battleships around the world as a powerful demonstration of the new U.S. role in the world. Above all, he felt certain that American know-how could solve any problem. Roosevelt, an admirer remarked, was "a steam engine in trousers."

Roosevelt's nation stood on the precipice of profound change. In 1900, at the turn of the century, the United States already ranked as the world's leading industrial power, but it was still essentially rural in character. Agriculture was the main livelihood, and some 60 percent of the 76 million people lived on farms or in small towns. Horses vastly outnumbered the new-fangled horseless carriage 21 million to 8,000. One in seven homes had a bathtub, one in 12 had a telephone, and one in 12 was wired for electricity. Even the visionaries of the day who believed that in their lifetime people would fly or women would serve in Congress could not have dreamed how vastly different their nation would be a hundred years hence.

The 125 events depicted in this book illustrate many of the happenings that have transformed America since 1900. Arranged chronologically as a timeline of the century, each event marks a milestone of change in realms such as science and technology, government, the nation's role in the world, the economy, the women's movement, or civil rights. Some of these events—two catastrophic world wars, the Great Depression, putting a man in space—scream out their overwhelming significance. Others, though seemingly trivial by comparison, merit inclusion for their impact on everyday American culture. For example, the very first event—the introduction of the Kodak Brownie camera in 1900—was a pioneering example of what historian Daniel Boorstin calls the American penchant for "mass-producing the moment." The Brownie allowed millions of 20th-century Americans to record their experiences and then endlessly relive them. Finally, although the perspective of this book is principally American, it also looks at events from around the world, such as Adolf Hitler's rise to power in 1933, that have had profound effects on the nation's destiny.

The New Frontier: Despite the ebullience of political leaders like Teddy Roosevelt, many national leaders were concerned at the turn of the century by the closing of the western frontier. With the filling up of the continent's vast open spaces, they feared that opportunity would disappear. But another kind of frontier that required little land opened up and flourished early in the new century. American know-how fostered a revolution in technological innovation and in the methods of mass production. Henry Ford's development of the moving automobile assembly line in 1913

Receptive to the modern but in no hurry to abandon the past, a resourceful American takes advantage of old-fashioned horsepower to extricate his vehicle from the spring mud.

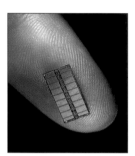

Since their invention in 1958, memory chips like the model displayed above on a fingertip have doubled in capacity and have fallen in price by half every 18 months or so.

pioneered manufacturing systems that turned out every conceivable product uniformly and efficiently.

Through the automobile and other advanced forms of transportation, technology almost immediately began to shrink the vast distances that separated American communities. The primitive gasoline engine that powered the flights of Orville and Wilbur Wright in 1903 was separated by four decades from the jet engine and a mere 66 years from the rocket power that plunked astronauts Neil Armstrong and Buzz Aldrin down on the dusty moon in 1969.

Even more stunning than rapid transportation was the development of ever faster and more powerful ways to transmit and receive information. The telephone and the radio replaced the telegraph for long-distance communication. Radio became a commercial broadcasting medium in 1920, and three decades later, television was making its way into the American home.

By the final decade of the century, however, the key to making information available quickly was the digital computer and the chips that powered it. The first giant computers after World War II filled entire rooms. Then the tiny transistor, invented in 1947, replaced the fragile, bulky vacuum tubes in switching and amplifying electric currents. In 1958, scientists combined several transistors with other components in a single integrated circuit, or chip. In 1997, as many as five million transistors could be crammed onto a chip the size of a fingernail, and scientists were predicting

that number to rise to 18 million in less than a decade. These mighty mites made everything electronic work, from wristwatches to washing machines, from automobile ignitions to the space shuttle, from supercomputers to the personal computer, which was far more commonplace in the American home at century's end than the telephone had been in 1900.

The speed-up in the dissemination of information can be seen vividly in two events not much more than a century apart. In 1865, news of Abraham Lincoln's assassination required 12 days by ship to reach London. In 1997, the radio signals that programmers at supercomputers on the ground in California used to manipulate the movements of the *Sojourner* robot 200 million miles away on Mars arrived in 10 minutes. Ordinary Americans, sitting at home in front of their personal computers, could log on to the Internet and become citizens of the galactic village as they watched extraterrestrial images of a Martian sunset sent back by the robot.

Reluctant Superpower: It was largely by wielding the big stick of technology that the United States gained an ever larger place in world affairs. This ascendancy was marked by tension between traditional American isolationism, heeding George Washington's and Thomas Jefferson's admonitions about the dangers of foreign alliances, and the opposing desire to assert ourselves internationally. At the turn of the century, the United States already had established itself as a world power during the Spanish-American War of 1898. That "splendid little war," as Secretary of State John Hay had characterized it, had confirmed our dominance in the Western Hemisphere by capturing Cuba and Puerto Rico and established a foothold in the Pacific by taking the Philippines and other islands. Despite Teddy Roosevelt's forays onto the international stage, American isolationism remained so powerful that President Woodrow Wilson had to rely on our missionary spirit—our vision of ourselves as the torchbearers of democracy—to take the nation into World War I in 1917.

After that first decisive intervention in Europe, Americans retreated from international politics to trade as the basis of for-

weaponry. On August 6, 1945, an atomic bomb exploded over the Japanese city of Hiroshima, helping push the fighting to a conclusion and inaugurating the nuclear age.

The threat of nuclear annihilation prevailed throughout the subsequent Cold War between the United States and its erstwhile ally, the Soviet Union. The U.S.S.R.'s collapse in 1989 left the United States as the world's lone superpower. It was a nation fully capable of intervening decisively in conflicts such as the Gulf War in 1991, though still retaining much of the old reluctance to act as the world's policeman.

Bill Clinton savors the fruit of American intervention in world affairs as traditional archenemies—Israeli prime minister Yitzhak Rabin (left) and Palestine Liberation Organization chairman Yasser Arafat—shake hands in 1993.

"What Rome was to the ancient world, and Great Britain has been to the modern world, America is to be to the world tomorrow."

Walter Lippmann, columnist, 1945

---

eign relations. The rise of totalitarian states in Germany, Japan, and Italy threatened global stability during the 1930s. After the outbreak of World War II the United States became the "arsenal of democracy," supplying weapons to Great Britain and the Soviet Union, but it took the direct Japanese attack on Pearl Harbor in 1941 to jolt the country into war. The urgency of the war spurred U.S. technology to the far edge of

Bigger Government: When Teddy Roosevelt was inaugurated in 1901, the federal government was spending a little over $500 million a year. The citizenry tended to look to local and state government rather than to Washington to deal with economic and social issues. But the need to rein in the burgeoning power of big business led Roosevelt to use his self-described "bully pulpit" to articulate many principles of the reformers who called themselves progressives. The progressive movement took on a broad range of issues, supporting, among other things, antitrust actions, prohibition, labor laws to protect women and children, and the 17th Amendment to the Constitution, which furthered democracy by mandating election of U.S. senators by the voters rather than by state legislatures.

Perhaps the most far-reaching reform was the 16th Amendment, authorizing the imposition of a tax on income, for it provided a constitutional means to finance the growth of the federal government. The federal income tax, enacted in 1913, called for a modest levy of 1 percent on personal income exceeding $3,000 and 7 percent on incomes above $500,000. Less than 1 percent of the population had to pay, and the form they filed was only one page long.

The federal government took a far more active role in the economy when the Great Depression of the 1930s forced a renewal of the progressive spirit. Desperate for relief from unemployment that soared above 25 percent, Americans looked to Washington and another Roosevelt, who was Teddy's distant cousin. Promising "a new deal," President Franklin D. Roosevelt pushed through programs that gave the federal government unprecedented powers. He offered such innovations as a minimum wage, unemployment insurance, and social security. Subsequent presidents and con-

gresses continued to enlarge the federal role in the economy, education, science, medicine, and other realms once considered off-limits to Washington.

The appropriate scope of the federal government in American life was increasingly subject to debate toward the end of the century. But even such a professed conservative as President Ronald Reagan, who often spoke of government as the problem rather than the solution, did not seek to fundamentally reduce federal power. In fact, Washington took on new responsibilities. The growing awareness of the need to protect the environment from the ravages of technological progress, for instance, resulted in the regulation of land, air, and water. Such efforts harked back to Teddy Roosevelt, who declared, "I hate the man who would skin the land!" A vigorous promoter of environmental conservation, he set aside two million acres for national parks and wildlife refuges and another 148 million acres for national forests—an area almost the size of the state of Texas.

Nation on the Move: Where Americans lived underwent a tremendous shift, a trend hastened by technology. Tractors and other machines transformed agriculture, reducing the number of farmworkers needed and sending them to cities in search of economic opportunity. At the same time, the automobile was giving Americans an amazing mobility. There were 6,771,000 passenger cars in the United States in 1919, and by 1929 the number was up to 23,121,000—

Set aside by Congress "for the benefit and enjoyment of the people," Yellowstone National Park draws more than three million visitors a year with attractions like the famous Old Faithful geyser (above).

one car for about every five Americans. Local, state, and federal governments were making it much easier for people to get where they wanted or needed to go. During the 1920s alone, more than 600,000 miles of roads were built to accommodate the auto and link new and old urban areas. This accomplishment was as significant in its day as the construction of the Interstate Highway System launched in 1956.

One of the largest internal mass migrations in the world's history occurred among black Americans. In 1900, nearly 90 percent of the black population lived in the South, mostly in the countryside. Their exodus began during World War I, when industrialists sent agents south to recruit workers for their northern factories. Even so, as late as 1940, 77 percent of blacks still lived in the South. During World War II, many moved north to work in weapons factories in Detroit, Chicago, and other cities. But the pivotal event was the widespread introduction during the 1940s of the mechanical cotton picker. Even an early model could take the place of 50 workers, and by 1970, no fewer than five million southern blacks had moved to the urban North.

Another migration, overwhelmingly white, was taking place meanwhile. The demand for housing by GIs returning home from World War II generated a tremendous growth of new suburbs around the cities. During the 1950s alone, the stock of U.S. housing increased by one-third. Soon more than one-third of the population was living in suburbia, shopping in suburban malls and commuting to work, irrevocably committed to the automobile as a way of life.

Sharing the Dream: Everything from the affordable automobile to the fast-food hamburger rolled off the American-style assembly line. The system of mass production that Henry Ford originated was highly efficient—and highly profitable. Instead of passing the lion's share of the profits on to stockholders, Ford chose to increase his workers' wages. With more disposable income, they could afford to buy the low-cost cars they were manufacturing and consequently increased the demand.

However, a workingman had to save up the entire purchase price for the car before he could drive it away. Then, in 1915, the installment plan for buying became widely available for the first time, and the would-be consumer no longer had to delay his gratification. Installment buying was originally devised for the automobile market, but soon people were able to buy everything from radios to refrigerators on time.

Installment buying—along with seductive advertisements for goods that had once been unattainable luxuries for the working class and much of the middle class—multiplied the universe of customers, which was exactly what mass producers needed. Mass production and mass consumption were necessary companions,

Participants in the great wave of migration that carried hundreds of thousands of African Americans north between 1915 and 1950, a southern boy and his mother pose behind their well-packed car.

a two-part invention that transformed the nation's economy and allowed ever increasing numbers of Americans to share in the dream of material abundance.

The consumer economy shifted into high gear during the second half of the century. Going without during the Depression and World War II generated an immense pent-up demand for consumer goods. The United States produced as much between 1950 and 1965 as it had during the entire period since the founding of the Jamestown colony in 1607.

A Woman's Place: At the turn of the century, half of the population—women—did not enjoy the right to vote under the U.S. Constitution. Middle-class women rarely worked outside the home, to which they were bound by motherhood and domestic chores. A woman's place beyond the home remained subject to other issues. When jobs were scarce during the 1930s, a Gallup poll found a 78 percent disapproval of a married woman working outside the home if her husband was capable of supporting her. Patriotism dictated that women work in factories during World War II—and then make way for the returning GIs. Women— some eagerly, some with reluctance and regret—returned to domesticity full-time. Taking the approved role of mother seriously, they had babies at a clip that raised the country's birthrate 50 percent.

The baby boom was still going on when

Women link arms and march for equal rights on Fifth Avenue in New York on August 26, 1970, 50 years to the day after the 19th Amendment was added to the U.S. Constitution, granting them the right to vote.

the birth-control pill came on the market, allowing women to determine with far greater reliability than ever before when or whether to bear a child. And in 1973, the Supreme Court decision in *Roe v. Wade* guaranteed the right to terminate pregnancy. Meanwhile, the publication of Betty Friedan's *Feminine Mystique* in 1963 raised profound questions about women in American society and launched a movement that would reverberate throughout the rest of the century in home and workplace.

Who Is an American? One of the most pronounced trends of the century was the widening embrace of democratic principles and ideals. "We have a great desire to be supremely American," commented President Calvin Coolidge in 1925. But far too often national identity—who was or was not an American—was defined in racial, ethnic, religious, or political terms. During the 1920s, the Ku Klux Klan stirred hatred against Catholics, Jews, and recent immigrants as well as black citizens. Anti-Semitism subsided after revelations of the Holocaust, and John F. Kennedy proved in 1960 that a Catholic could be elected president. But persisting bias against Asians led to the internment of 110,000 Japanese Americans during World War II. By contrast, Americans of German and Italian extraction were typically left alone.

It was not religion, national origin, or sex but the issue of skin color that was central to the century's greatest struggle over who was a full and free American. In 1900, most black Americans were only 35 years removed from slavery. But they were still shackled throughout the South by laws that, with approval from the U.S. Supreme Court in *Plessy v. Ferguson* in 1896, segregated public accommodations ranging from schools to water fountains under the concept of "separate but equal."

Like so much political, economic, and social change in America, the pivotal period in the battle for black civil rights came after World War II. In 1948, after blacks had fought in segregated units during two world wars, President Harry Truman issued Exec-

All Americans: Much remained to be done, but the expansion of American democracy within our own borders surely ranked among the outstanding achievements of the century. One measure of change was the fact that by the end of the century women and blacks, Jews, Catholics, and Italians had sat on the Supreme Court. Society, moreover, was increasingly sensitive to and tolerant of the differences that characterize Americans in gender, religion, sexual orientation, and ethnic or racial heritage. With the tendency to respect the differences in people came a recognition of their similari-

Golfer Tiger Woods took the sporting world by storm since turning professional in 1996, winning four of the first 16 tournaments he entered and becoming the youngest Masters champion ever.

"And this nation, for all its hopes and boasts, will not be fully free until all its citizens are free."

John F. Kennedy, 1963

utive Order 9981 directing desegregation of the armed forces. More victories followed, including the Supreme Court's 1954 ban on segregation in America's public schools. But it took the courage and persistence of the many blacks and some whites who risked their lives in nonviolent protest to finally secure the legal underpinnings of racial justice. In 1960, black college students staged a sit-in at a lunch counter in Greensboro, North Carolina, inaugurating a decade of political activism by the young. Out of such turbulence grew congressional legislation outlawing discrimination in public facilities and ensuring voting rights for all.

ties and a refusal to arbitrarily pigeonhole them. Thanks to immigration and integration, we became a nation in which individual heritages cut across and transcended old barriers.

A much publicized case in point occurred near the end of the century, in 1997, when the young golfer Tiger Woods won the Masters tournament at the extraordinary age of 21. Woods refused to be categorized as an African American. He was, he said, one-eighth Caucasian, one-fourth black, one-eighth American Indian, one-fourth Thai, and one-fourth Chinese. And, his many admirers might have added, *all* American.

Immigrant children climb aboard an all-American wagon at an Ellis Island playground around 1910.

The Events

★

1900 Cameras for All

When George Eastman took up photography, the process required a hundred-dollar "pack-horse load" of equipment. He tackled the problem, and in 1888 introduced the Kodak camera—a 26-

> "So simple they can be easily operated by any school boy or girl."
>
> Brownie advertisement, 1900

ounce, easy-to-use marvel. At 25 dollars, however, it was too costly for most families, as were several later models. Then, in 1900, Eastman brought out the one-dollar Brownie, named for the sprites in a popular children's book. More than 100,000 sold the first year. Not everyone appreciated the change Eastman had wrought. "Now every nipper has a Brownie," complained one photographer. "And a photograph is as common as a box of matches."

With a Brownie camera, ordinary Americans could document any occasion and immortalize friends and relatives, as shown in these snapshots from the early 1900s.

Sold in a colorful box (left), the Brownie camera (below) appealed to children. A roll of film for the original model cost just 15 cents.

1901
The Birth of U.S. Steel

Steel tycoon Andrew Carnegie, who went to work in a cotton mill when he was a poor immigrant boy, was by 1901 one of the richest men in the world. He was also ready to retire, and he struck a deal with one of his chief competitors, the powerful financier John Pierpont Morgan, to sell his empire for more than $400 million. Morgan combined Carnegie Steel with his own Federal Steel and 10 other companies to create the United States Steel Corporation.

Morgan's creation was the nation's first billion-dollar corporation. On March 3, 1901, the day the merger was announced, it was valued at $1.4 billion, an amount nearly double the cost of running the federal government for a single year. U.S. Steel controlled almost two thirds of the nation's steel market, and some saw its near monopoly as a danger to democracy. The president of Yale University predicted that unless U.S. Steel and other big companies were regulated, there would be "an emperor in Washington within twenty-five years." But U.S. Steel stocks soared, bought by enthusiastic speculators across the country. "Even in thrifty Western towns and New England country villages, the gossip of an evening was apt to concern itself with 'Steel,' " recalled one observer a few years later.

Andrew Carnegie, meanwhile, distributed much of his fortune to colleges, libraries, and foundations. He could have had even more to give away. After the merger, Carnegie told Morgan he should have set the price for his company $100 million higher. The financier replied, "If you had, I should have paid it."

Carnegie Steel executives celebrate the birth of U.S. Steel at a table shaped like a steel rail. The corporation owned everything from iron ore mines to railroads and ships.

> "The time has come for the National League and the American League to organize a World Series."

Pittsburgh team owner Barney Dreyfuss, 1903

1903
The First World Series

In 1901, baseball's 25-year-old National League got a brash new competitor—the American League, which lured players away from the older organization by offering them an average increase of $500 a year. After two years of squabbling over players and territories, the two leagues made peace and sealed it by organizing a World Series. The best-of-nine contest between the National League's Pittsburgh Pirates and the American League's Boston Pilgrims (later the Red Sox) drew tens of thousands of fans, who often surged onto the field, stopping play.

Boston's supporters sang the tune "Tessie" over and over again, improvising such lines as "Jimmy, you know I love you madly" for a Boston player and "Honus, why do you hit so badly," for Pittsburgh's Honus Wagner. The song "sort of got on your nerves after a while," recalled Wagner's teammate third baseman Tommy Leach. "And before we knew what happened, we'd lost the World Series."

More likely, it was the pitching. With two Pittsburgh pitchers out of action, Deacon Phillippe stood almost alone against Boston aces Bill Dinneen and Cy Young. Phillippe pitched—and won—three of the first four games, then rested as Pittsburgh lost games five and six, tying the series. In an exhausting feat, he pitched two more games, but was unable to win either. With the series clinched at 5-3, Boston fans carried their players to the dressing room as the stands "swayed and rocked with the might salvos of applause," reported the *Boston Post.* Following a break in 1904, the World Series resumed, delivering a century-spanning sequence of heroic contests unequaled in American sports.

Ball used in 1903 World Series, game 8

1903 World Series ticket

Boston vs. Pittsburg

3

ADMISSION
RAIN CHECK

VOID AFTER
5 INNINGS ARE PLAYED

On the last day of the series, Pittsburgh players pose for a group portrait with the American League's victorious Boston team.

Fans pour onto the field at Boston's Huntington Avenue Baseball Grounds (right) after Pittsburgh's 4-2 win over Boston in game 3. The cheapest seat cost 50 cents, twice the amount charged for the season's regular games.

1903
First in Flight

It was December 17; ice coated the puddles on the beach near Kitty Hawk, North Carolina. But Wilbur Wright *(above, left)* and his brother Orville wanted to test their Flyer despite the cold. After four years of work in their Ohio bicycle shop and repeated trips to Kitty Hawk—chosen for its high winds, unobstructed space, and soft, impact-absorbing sands—the brothers were determined to become the first human beings to fly a heavier-than-air craft.

With the Flyer at one end of a 60-foot track, Orville took the controls, lying prone to reduce air resistance. The 12-horsepower engine chattered as the biplane rolled into the wind. Forty feet along, moving at seven miles an hour, it took off, reaching a height of 10 feet. Under Orville's guidance the Flyer dipped, climbed, dipped, and landed, all in 12 seconds. It had flown 120 feet. Orville and Wilbur took turns flying three more times. Then, as they were putting it away, a wintry gust of wind smashed the Flyer too badly for on-site repairs.

It took six more years of work before the brothers gained world renown and began to enjoy commercial success. Wilbur died of typhoid in 1912, but Orville lived until 1948, witnessing the birth of airmail, fighter planes, aerial bombing, commercial airlines, and jets. For him, however, the real excitement had come much earlier. "I got more thrill out of flying before I had ever been in the air at all," he once told a visitor, "lying in bed thinking how exciting it would be to fly."

As Wilbur watches, Orville Wright pilots the Flyer

Orville Wright was 32 and Wilbur was 36 when they successfully demonstrated the world's first airplane. Orville telegraphed the news (right) to their father back in Ohio.

RECEIVED at   170

176 C KA CS 33 Paid.   Via Norfolk Va

Kitty Hawk N C Dec 17

Bishop M Wright

          7 Hawthorne St

Success four flights thursday morning all against twenty one mile
wind started from Level with engine power alone average speed
through air thirty one miles longest 57 seconds inform Press
home three Christmas .   Orevelle Wright   525P

in the first powered flight of a heavier-than-air craft. A witness from the local lifesaving station took the picture.

1904
Ice Cream Cone Invented

Immigrants have bestowed countless culinary delights on the United States, but none surpasses the ice-cream cone as a national institution. The treat traces its origins to a sweltering day at the St. Louis World's Fair of 1904, when unusually heavy business at an ice-cream stand caused it to run out of paper dishes. A nearby vendor named Ernest Hamwi, originally from Damascus, Syria, had the idea of taking flat pastries called zalabia and twisting them into cones to use in place of dishes. Dubbed the World's Fair Cornucopia, the ice-cream-filled pastry proved to be a great hit with the fairgoers.

The ice-cream cone snowballed into a mass market treat when an engineer produced a cone-rolling machine in 1909. The invention was inspired by his experience at the St. Louis fair, where he had been among the many who enjoyed the new-fangled World's Fair Cornucopia. It was an idea whose time had come.

1906
The San Francisco Earthquake

Just after dawn on April 18, an earthquake tore through San Francisco. "I could see it actually coming up Washington Street," policeman Jesse Cook recalled. "The whole street was undulating. It was as if the waves of the ocean were coming towards me."

Downtown San Francisco lies in ruins in this scene captured by local resident J. B.

In seconds, the quake collapsed buildings, twisted cable-car tracks, ruptured water mains and gas lines, and tore down electric wires. Fires flared up across the city. With little water available for fighting the blazes, they burned for three days, destroying almost five square miles of buildings at the city's core. In all, 315 people were known dead and another 352 were missing.

The resilient survivors were soon cracking jokes ("Ring bell for landlady," read a sign on one burned-out family's tent), organizing relief efforts, and rebuilding. Three years later 20,000 buildings, constructed mainly of brick and steel to new fire codes, had risen from the rubble. The city also improved its ability to keep water flowing in the event of another devastating earthquake.

Monaco, whose wife and son somberly huddle together in the foreground at right.

1906
Reforming
an Industry

When crusading journalist Upton Sinclair wrote *The Jungle*, he intended for the plight of his novel's hero, a Lithuanian immigrant working in a Chicago stockyard, to arouse sympathy for all exploited workers of the meat-packing industry. Drawing on his own undercover investigation, Sinclair described filthy, dangerous working conditions and such stomach-churning practices as processing meat from tubercular cattle and doctoring rotten meat with chemicals.

Sinclair's exposé sparked a huge outcry. After a government report confirmed his findings, meat sales dropped by half, and Congress quickly passed the Pure Food and Drug Act and the Meat Inspection Act. It was a big step forward for consumers—but no measures to protect industry workers were forthcoming. "I aimed at the public's heart," Sinclair later wrote, "and by accident I hit it in the stomach."

Immigrants flow through a welcoming arch toward a sun bearing the words "Progress and Prosperity" in this 1903 cartoon. The books, slate, and sponge eraser under Uncle Sam's arm link progress to education.

"That's all you heard: Gold on the streets of America. It was all good things. You could be anything you want here and make a lot of money, even if it was a dollar a day."

A Polish immigrant

1907
The High Tide of Immigration

Between 1880 and 1924 more than 26 million immigrants came to America. The peak year was 1907, when more than 1.2 million newcomers entered, the vast majority through the immigration center of Ellis Island in New York Harbor. Fleeing poverty and sometimes religious or ethnic persecution, these desperate yet optimistic people abandoned everything they knew in hopes of making a better life in the United States. A woman explaining her decision to pull up stakes said that "we didn't have anything to do in Ireland, there was no work. And you didn't want to be poor all your life. . . . So I said, 'Goodbye, I'll see you later.'"

Most immigrants traveled in steerage, paying around $30 for a ticket. They spent most of their hours in open dormitories packed with hundreds of bunk beds. There was little privacy belowdecks, and in stormy weather seasickness made the close quarters even more unpleasant. Recalling her six-week passage from Russia in 1908, one woman said, "Everyone had smelly food, and the atmosphere was so thick and dense with smoke and bodily odors that your head itched, and when you went to scratch your head you got lice in your hands."

The first hours after landing were a mixture of exhilaration, anxiety, and confusion. Newcomers had to pass the dreaded Immigration Service inspection, which made sure they were healthy, had at least some money, and could support themselves. "Every so often somebody called out names," an Eastern European man recalled of the wait on Ellis Island. "I was very nervous because it was so noisy.

Steerage passengers jam the deck of the S.S. Patricia as it arrives in New York in 1906. Russian-born Gertrude Yellin's eagerness to be in America "was so great and so sunny, that it colored all the pain we had during our trip."

I couldn't hear the names and I was afraid that I would miss my name and remain there forever." The immigration officers were brusquely efficient. "Wherever you were pushed, that's where you went," one arrival said. "The only thing that kept me going was that right across the water you could see the land of golden opportunity." Despite anxieties about being turned away, the chances of such a misfortune were slight: Ninety-eight percent of immigrants were cleared to enter the country.

Although by 1910 nearly one out of every seven Americans was foreign born, newcomers often faced resentment, suspicion, and prejudice. After World War I a growing aversion to foreigners swept the country, and a quota system began to close the open-door policy, ending the largest mass migration in history. By then, the millions who had left the Old World to pursue the American dream had enriched the texture of national life and changed their new home forever.

"My mother had to try to keep track of us. She finally took us and tied us all together so that we would stay together. And that's the way we came off the boat."

A Swiss immigrant

Fresh off the boat in 1905, the kerchiefed woman at left puts her son in charge of his little sister. To mark a red-letter day in their lives, many immigrants put on their best clothes before disembarking.

Canvas satchel from Switzerland

Swedish high-top shoes

Wooden trunk from Italy

Swiss girl's teddy bear

1909
Freud in America

American notions about the mind were never quite the same after the September celebration of the 20th anniversary of Clark University in Worcester, Massachusetts. The guest lecturer, little known in the United States until then, was Sigmund Freud. Speaking in German, Freud explained his radical theory that most nervous disorders could be traced to repressed, often sexual, thoughts

hidden in the unconscious. To Freud's delight, the audience of eminent scholars was fascinated. Proudly, he posed for a portrait with colleagues A. A. Brill *(top left)* and Ernest Jones *(top right)* and Clark president G. Stanley Hall *(bottom right)*. Psychoanalysis, as Freud called his approach, not only transformed American psychology but also influenced the work of artists and writers such as surrealist painter Salvador Dali and playwright Eugene O'Neill.

1911
A Fiery Horror

Work had just ended at the Triangle Shirtwaist Factory on Saturday, March 25, when fire broke out in a heap of scraps. Packed into the top three floors of a 10-story Manhattan building, 500 workers—many of them young immigrant women—desperately tried to find a way out. "I broke the window of the elevator door with my hands and screamed 'Fire! Fire! Fire!' " one woman recalled of her desperate attempt to get the car to stop at her floor. "It was so hot we could scarcely breathe." Those who couldn't get to an elevator made for the roof, narrow stairways, or the single fire escape, which collapsed; some could only reach the windows. "Dozens of girls were hanging from the ledges," a policeman

Families search for loved ones among the dead. The average age of the victims was 19.

recalled. "Others, their dresses on fire, were leaping from the windows." Firefighters sprayed the building with water during and after the fire *(right),* but their ladders could not reach the affected floors.

In all, 146 workers died in the fire, many the sole financial support of their families. About 400,000 attended a funeral march to honor the victims, and an angry city demanded justice as investigations showed dangerously crowded working conditions, a lack of sprinklers or fire drills, inadequate fire escapes, and strong evidence of locked doors. One newspaper ran a gallows each day on the front page captioned "This Ought to Fit Somebody; Who Is He?" When the factory owners were found not guilty of manslaughter, public outrage increased, helping to produce 36 workplace safety laws in New York State and inspiring similar reforms elsewhere.

1913
The Armory Show

Although two-thirds of the artists who exhibited at the Armory Show were American, the poster at left gives top billing to Europeans like Matisse whose works sparked the most debate. When the show traveled to Chicago, outraged art students stabbed an effigy of the painter and burned a copy of his Blue Nude (below).

For most Americans, their first chance to see the work of such avant-garde European artists as Cézanne, Gauguin, Matisse, and Picasso came when an exhibit of 1,300 pieces of modern art opened in New York City's 69th Regiment Armory. Some 90,000 visitors flocked to the Armory Show, and another 200,000 attended smaller versions in Chicago and Boston.

Viewers reacted strongly, some with shock and dismay, others with excitement. Marcel Duchamp's cubist painting *Nude Descending a Staircase,* shown at far right, was among the show's major attractions. Many critics, however, were offended by the abstract, robotlike figure, and one of them fumed that it looked like "a pack of brown cards in a nightmare." Henri Matisse's works also provoked spectators, including one who found his paintings "revolting in their humanity." However, the Armory Show did inspire many homegrown artists to experiment with abstraction, fulfilling the prophecy made by the *New York Globe*'s reviewer: "American art will never be the same again."

> ## "American art will never be the same again."
>
> *New York Globe*

One wag called Constantin Brancusi's Mlle. Pagany (above) "a hard-boiled egg balanced on a cube of sugar." Another renamed the cubist room, which featured Marcel Duchamp's Nude Descending a Staircase (below) and other works, the "Chamber of Horrors."

Henry Ford, shown here in 1913, used efficiency experts to detect and eliminate assembly-line workers' waste motions.

1913
Ford's Assembly Line

Henry Ford's first Model T was a fine car—rugged, reliable, easy to repair. But Ford had made it his mission to build a motor car "for the great multitude," and at $825 when it went on sale in 1908, the Model T was out of the multitude's reach. Ford turned his ingenuity to streamlining mass production, and in 1913 he put a revolutionary innovation into operation—a continuously moving assembly line. Ford borrowed the basic idea from the meat-packing industry, in which overhead trolleys delivered carcasses to the workers. In Ford's version, workers were stationed along waist-level assembly lines carrying incomplete

chassis or components. The assembly process had been divided into many small operations, and each worker performed just one of these little jobs all day long on every passing component or chassis. "The man who puts in a bolt does not put on the nut," Ford explained. "The man who puts on the nut does not tighten it." So efficient was this division of labor that in 1913 a Model T was assembled in one-eighth the time required in 1908, and its price was $300 lower.

Ford continued to shave time off the process and to pass on the savings, lopping another $25 off the Model T's price tag in 1914. "Every time I reduce the charge for our car by $1.00, I get a thousand new buyers," he said. Greater efficiency and rising sales meant more profits, and in a step that excited national admiration, in 1914 Ford shared some of those profits by doubling the average wage he paid to five dollars a day. With more money in their pockets, Ford workers could afford Model Ts of their own and enjoy firsthand the mobility that was beginning to transform the nation.

"I will build a motor car for the great multitude."

Henry Ford, 1907

Ready for their bodies to be bolted on, one thousand Model T chassis are lined up outside Ford's Highland Park factory, where the first continuously moving assembly line was installed. In 1908, the first year of production, more than 10,000 Model Ts were sold. By 1920 nearly 4,000,000 were on the road, accounting for half the cars in the world.

1914 Model T touring car

Around the World

1914
Two Deaths
Start a War

During the late 1800s, Austria-Hungary gained control of Bosnia and Herzegovina, two of the Balkan states of southern Europe. Nearby Serbia, however, remained independent—and a source of hope for bitter residents of the two subjugated territories. On June 28, 1914, six men who dreamed of a "Greater Serbia" gathered in the Bosnian capital of Sarajevo to kill the visiting heir to the throne of Austria-Hungary, Archduke Francis Ferdinand. A first attempt failed, but 19-year-old Gavrilo Princip got an unexpected second chance when the archduke's car stopped and backed up. Princip fired, fatally wounding the archduke and his wife, Sophie (above). On July 28, Austria-Hungary declared war on Serbia. Preexisting alliances drew in almost every European country, and World War I began.

1915
A Movie Milestone

For three hours, the audience at the Los Angeles premiere of *The Birth of a Nation* sat spellbound, then rose to applaud wildly at the film's conclusion. D. W. Griffith's epic tale of the Civil War far surpassed any feature film they had ever seen before in storytelling power and sheer artfulness. Using closeups, fade-ins, crosscutting, extreme long shots, and other innovations, Griffith wove a complex narrative that magically blended spectacle and intimacy.

Moviegoers all over the country were dazzled by *The Birth of a Nation.* "It is like writing history with lightning," said President Woodrow Wilson. Many Americans, however, were deeply offended by the racial attitudes of the film, which depicted black characters as childlike and potentially savage and portrayed the Ku Klux Klan sympathetically. The fledgling National Association for the Advancement of Colored People sought injunctions against the film in several cities, arguing it could inflame racial tensions. But some NAACP members

Griffith uses a megaphone on the set of an early movie.

ruefully attested to Griffith's mesmerizing skill as a storyteller, admitting that they had been swept away while his cinematic spectacle unfolded before their eyes.

Though in some ways deplorable, *The Birth of a Nation* became the touchstone for feature films. At Griffith's death in 1948, the great French director René Clair said, "Nothing essential has been added to the cinema since Griffith."

The Fiery Cross of the Ku Klux Klan —

D.W. GRIFFITH'S **MIGHTY SPECTACLE**
THE BIRTH OF A NATION
FOUNDED ON THOMAS DIXON'S 'THE CLANSMAN'

A Klansman is glorified on the movie poster above.

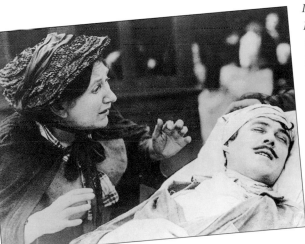

In a closeup from The Birth of a Nation, a visitor to a military hospital hovers anxiously over a wounded officer. Director Griffith said that the closeup allowed him to "photograph thought."

1916
Self-Service Shopping

Before Clarence Saunders opened the first Piggly Wiggly grocery store in Memphis, Tennessee, shoppers were used to waiting in line to make their purchases. The customer at the front of the line handed a clerk a shopping list; the clerk located each item, laboriously measuring and packaging flour and other products sold in bulk, and rang up the sale. Then it was the next person's turn. At Piggly Wiggly, on the other hand, shoppers could scoop up a handbasket and head down aisles of packaged goods, choose what they liked, and then pay a cashier at the turnstile exit.

Saunder's system of "self-service" proved popular with retailers and consumers alike because it made stores cheaper to operate and more convenient to shop at. The idea was first borrowed by other grocers, then spread to stores selling other kinds of goods. By the end of the century, even gas stations and banks—through automated teller machines (ATMs)—were arranged so that customers could serve themselves.

PIGGLY WIGGLY

1916
A Child
Labor Law

One of the ugliest aspects of U.S. industry was child labor. By 1913, 20 percent of American children, some only four or five years old, worked in mills, factories, and mines. Wages were as low as a dollar a day and the workday as long as 14 hours. In 1904, reformers founded the National Child Labor Committee. Among their greatest weapons were photos, including those shown here, taken by Lewis Hine, an NCLC investigator. The reform drive led to new state laws, and Congress passed the first national law in 1916, when it barred all goods made by workers under 14 from interstate commerce. But the battle was not over. Ruling that states had the right to regulate employment, the Supreme Court overturned the statute. It was not until 1938 that federal law prohibited the worst abuses of child laborers.

Vermont mill girl, age 12

Boys hired to pick debris from a chute of moving coal pose for Lewis Hine.

1917
"The Yanks Are Coming!"

In a famous World War I recruiting poster, America's Uncle Sam points a finger at potential soldiers.

With a rifle at his side, Private T. P. Laughlin of the U.S. Army's 42nd Division kisses his family goodbye before shipping out overseas.

To Americans at the start of the century, European politics were a distant affair. "An archduke more or less makes little difference," editorialized the *Grand Forks Daily Herald* after the assassination of Archduke Francis Ferdinand of Austria-Hungary *(page 56)*. When his death triggered World War I, Americans were shocked but glad not to be involved in the growing conflict between the Allies, which included Britain, France, Belgium, and Russia, and the Central Powers of Germany, Austria-Hungary, Bulgaria, and Turkey.

That attitude abruptly changed in 1915 with the sinking of the British passenger liner *Lusitania* by a German U-boat. Of the approximately 2,000 people on board, 1,198 died; 128 of the dead were American. Despite public outcry, President Woodrow Wilson reached a settlement with Germany, which pledged to pull back its submarines. "There is such a thing as a man being too proud to fight," Wilson said.

America stopped being too proud in mid-March when German U-boats sank four U.S. cargo ships. When Wilson asked for a declaration of war on April 2, Congress erupted in cheers. Four days later, Broadway's George M. Cohan composed "Over There," which became the unofficial anthem of the war, with its stirring refrain "The Yanks Are Coming!"

Despite the excitement, the U.S. was woefully unprepared. Its army numbered only about 200,000 troops, and it

The use of poison gases by both sides made gas masks like those worn by the men of the 16th Infantry's First Division essential (right).

had fewer than 250 planes and no tanks. Wilson appointed officials to change all that. Financier Bernard Baruch organized industry into a war machine, and the nation's food administrator, Herbert Hoover, promoted voluntary rationing that included meatless Tuesdays to feed the troops. A new draft system registered nearly 10 million men on June 5, 1917, calling up the first 687,000 in late July.

By then, the vanguard of the American Expeditionary Force was in France. For most of the past three years, French, British, and Belgian troops had faced German soldiers along a 500-mile-long line of trenches. Now their new American comrades experienced the hell of trench warfare, a nightmarish combination of poison gas, nighttime barrages, sniper fire, rats, and pouring rain. "The war is a huge, killing beast that swallows up thousands and thousands of men in a single day," wrote an army private to his wife.

The strategic situation grew worse. Since the war began, Germany had been battling in the east with Russia. Outmatched, the Russians suffered crushing defeats until the unending loss of life and a weak economy combined to topple the monarchy in 1917. When the Communists seized power and agreed to a cease-fire with Germany in December, the German troops in the east were rushed west in hopes that they could break through

A recruitment poster pits an American eagle against a tattered war bird of imperial Germany to encourage flying aces to join the Army Air Service.

JOIN THE ARMY AIR SERVICE BE AN AMERICAN EAGLE!

CONSULT YOUR LOCAL DRAFT BOARD. READ THE ILLUSTRATED BOOKLET AT ANY RECRUITING OFFICE, OR WRITE TO THE CHIEF SIGNAL OFFICER OF THE ARMY, WASHINGTON, D. C.

An American soldier with a bandaged eye dictates a letter home to a Salvation Army worker. Of the estimated 10 million soldiers who died in the war, only 125,000 were American, many of whom were victims of influenza.

The shattered ruins of a French town bear mute witness to the war's devastation as a U.S. supply train files through in October 1918, just weeks before the conflict ended.

the Allied line before the full American force could arrive.

Pressed to the limit, the Allies held on—and the Americans continued to arrive, fresh and eager. In one famous battle, two marine regiments were instructed in June 1918 to retake Belleau Wood, a key strategic position. Early on, a French officer urged them to fall back from the vigorous German defense. "Retreat?" replied a marine captain. "Hell, we just got here." In just one day of fighting, there were 1,087 casualties—more than the Marine Corps had suffered in its entire 143-year history. But after three weeks they recaptured Belleau Wood.

The steady influx of Americans ultimately turned the tide. Late in 1918, the Allies broke the German line. The war ended on November 11.

America's role in World War I wrought sweeping changes. On the

Allied victory medal

world stage, the nation was a greater power than ever before. At home, it became more urban as thousands left farms and villages to work in wartime industries. The labor market of the war years had opened many jobs to women for the first time and sped up the movement of African Americans from the rural South to northern cities. The unprecedented prosperity generated by the war paved the way for the Roaring '20s.

Dressed patriotically in stars and stripes, a small boy watches as steel-helmeted Ameri-
previous wars from which soldiers returned home individually, World War I troops came

...can troops returning from overseas march down New York City's Fifth Avenue. Unlike ... back as entire units, and huge victory parades were held to celebrate their homecoming.

1919
A Dangerous Treaty

When President Wilson arrived in Europe for final peace negotiations, he was met by cheering crowds wherever he went (above). But Wilson's vision of a just settlement and a peaceful world community, embodied in his Fourteen Points proposal, was not embraced by the other Allies, who had suffered far greater losses and wanted to punish Germany severely. The final settlement, known as the Treaty of Versailles, did include Wilson's idea of a League of Nations, for which he later received the Nobel Peace Prize. But it also stripped Germany, the once proud imperial power, of all but 100,000 of its soldiers and set its war reparations at an impossible $32 billion. The humiliating terms —which were hotly resented by a young Austrian corporal named Adolf Hitler—led to an economic collapse in Germany and paved the way for the next world war.

1920
The Babe

When Boston Red Sox owner Harry Frazee traded his star pitcher to the New York Yankees on January 3, he made a big mistake. George Herman Ruth had won 89 games and lost 46 in six seasons for Boston, but he also hit home runs—lots of them. The Yanks put him in center field, and the 25-year-old Babe used his immense upper-body strength to slug 54 homers in 1920, 59 the next year, and an astounding 60 in 1927.

Babe Ruth changed baseball from a hit-and-run game played with a "dead ball" to an all-out power game. In doing so, he became the nation's first sports superstar, the Sultan of Swat. During the 1920 season fans learned that gamblers had bribed several Chicago White Sox players to throw the 1919 World Series. But just as the "Black Sox Scandal" tarnished the game, Ruth's popularity during the 1920s helped restore the reputation of the national pastime. And his prodigious ability created a legacy that has never been equaled.

"The only real game in the world, I think, is baseball."

Babe Ruth, 1947

Wherever he played, the Babe's swing was unmistakable. His philosophy of hitting was simple: "I swing as hard as I can, and I try to swing with everything I've got. I hit big or I miss big." He used the bat and well-worn glove shown below during his early years with the Yankees.

1920
Prohibition

On January 16, America went dry. The 18th Amendment to the U.S. Constitution declared that "the manufacture, sale, or transportation of intoxicating liquors within, the importation thereof into, or the exportation thereof from the United States . . . for beverage purposes is hereby prohibited." Farewell parties and mock funerals closed saloon doors across the land. The "Noble Experiment" had begun.

Widespread abuse of alcohol had been recognized as a serious social problem since colonial days, in rural America as well as in cities, and "demon rum" had long been condemned from many Protestant pulpits. But it took crusading women, most famously the hatchet-wielding Carry Nation, to assault the male stronghold of the saloon. "I tell you, ladies," said Nation to her disciples, "you don't know how much joy you will have until you begin to smash, smash, smash."

These crusaders, along with their male allies, used the Prohibition Party, the Women's Christian Temperance Union, and the Anti-Saloon League to coordinate the war on alcohol.

Twenty-six states, most of them in the Midwest and South, had banned the sale of alcohol by 1917, and during World War I alcohol production had been curtailed to reserve grain for food. At war's end, the prohibition movement kept the antiliquor momentum going, and the groundswell of public pressure, especially among suffragist women *(pages 70-71)*, pushed many reluctant politicians into backing the prohibition amendment that was submitted to Congress in 1917 and ratified by three-quarters of the states by 1919.

In the months before the 18th Amendment took effect, liquor merchants urged Americans to stockpile supplies against the dry times ahead. In fact, alcoholic beverages of all kinds were readily available throughout the 13 years the amendment was in effect.

Supporters of the Women's Christian Temperance Union parade their sentiments around 1915 (above). Besides being a champion of Prohibition, the WCTU fought to prohibit child labor (pages 58-59) and played a leading role in the woman suffrage movement (pages 70-71).

Although support was widespread, Prohibition had numerous vocal opponents, among them President Woodrow Wilson. He vetoed the Volstead Act, the law designed to enforce Prohibition, but Congress overrode his veto. Former president William Howard Taft predicted that "the business of manufacturing alcohol, liquor and beer will go out of the hands of law-abiding members of the community and will be transferred to the quasi-criminal classes."

Taft's warning was on target. While otherwise honest citizens learned to make modest amounts of gin, beer, or wine for their own private consumption, criminal entrepreneurs quenched the public's thirst with more than 70 million gallons of illicit alcohol a year (*opposite*). Most of it was manufactured in stills on U.S. soil, with a smaller amount smuggled in from Canada and the Caribbean. This bootleg booze was served up in clandestine bars called speakeasies. With the connivance of corrupt officials, illicit nightlife thrived on contraband liquor and the sheer thrill of flouting the law.

As time wore on, even ardent supporters of Prohibition had to admit that it was a failure. In 1933 Congress repealed the 18th Amendment, putting an end to the Noble Experiment.

In 1926, beer being dumped into Lake Michigan made headlines. Bootleg booze containing wood alcohol blinded, paralyzed, or killed thousands.

Alphonse
"Scarface"
Capone

Eliot Ness

Two Sides of the Law

Federal agent Eliot Ness and Chicago gangster Al Capone personified the extremes of Prohibition. Ness and his band of "Untouchables" spearheaded the effort to destroy the empire that Capone built on bootleg liquor. Prohibition was a golden opportunity for criminals, especially in the larger cities, where organized gangs took control of the beer and liquor traffic. The profits were huge: In 1927 alone, Capone's gang raked in some $60 million from bootlegging. Competing mobs routinely settled their differences with Tommy guns, and between 1920 and 1930 there were about 500 gangland murders in Chicago. Ness and his fellow agents raided secret warehouses and speakeasies, but their numbers were too small to keep pace with the gangsters. The federal government did manage to send Capone to prison for tax evasion in 1931, but organized crime had struck its roots so deep during Prohibition that it continued to prosper and grow after the 18th Amendment was repealed.

Stamps (above, left) and a poster represent the opposing positions in the long battle waged over a federal suffrage amendment. The first such amendment was introduced in Congress in 1868 by a senator from Kansas.

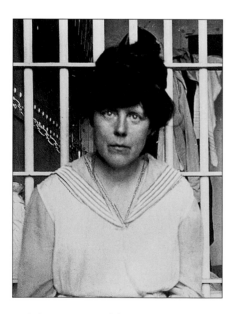

Activist Lucy Burns (above) headed many demonstrations in Washington and served more jail time than any other suffragist.

1920
Woman Suffrage

Begun at a convention in Seneca Falls, New York, in 1848, the campaign for woman suffrage demanded seven decades of struggle. Suffragists won their first real victory in 1869, when Wyoming, still a territory, gave women the vote. Other territories and states followed suit, but slowly—by 1917, women were voting in only 14 of the 48 states. The National Women's Party supported a constitutional amendment enfranchising every American

"We hold these truths to be self-evident: that all men and women are created equal."

Declaration of Sentiments, Seneca Falls, 1848

woman and picketed Woodrow Wilson's White House with banners demanding, "How long must women wait for liberty?"

Wilson reluctantly embraced their cause, and in 1919 Congress passed the suffrage amendment and submitted it to the states for ratification. The amendment was one state shy of the 36 needed for victory when the Tennessee legislature convened in August 1920. The deciding vote was cast by Harry Burn, whose constituents were largely antisuffrage. He was expected to vote nay, but on the morning of the vote he received a letter from his mother, Febb Ensminger Burn. "Hurrah, and vote for suffrage!" she wrote. Her words changed her son's mind—and, with it, the U.S. Constitution.

National Women's Party members display a banner quoting the crusading Susan B. Anthony at their Washington, D.C., headquarters (right).

1920
Commercial Radio

Eager to keep any technical advances in radio from slipping into enemy hands, the U.S. government banned all amateur experiments during World War I. When the prohibition was lifted late in 1919, experimental stations popped up across the country. One of these stations, 8XK in suburban Pittsburgh, was the brainchild of Westinghouse engineer Frank Conrad, who operated it from his home. He figured out how to air music from records played on an Edison phonograph, and while the music was playing he would travel to different spots around the city to check reception. Other wireless enthusiasts began picking up his broadcasts. As the word spread, Pittsburghers started building receivers from kits so they could listen in, and a department store that offered ready-made sets sold out.

Smelling a new opportunity, Westinghouse quickly hatched a plan to sell its own prebuilt radios. The company invited Conrad to move the station to the roof of its six-story Pittsburgh plant. Then, after obtaining a commercial license and the call letters KDKA from the U.S. Department of Commerce, the company made KDKA's maiden broadcast on November 2 into a media event by airing live the results of that day's presidential election pitting Democrat James M. Cox against Republican Warren G. Harding. The broadcast launched the age of commercial radio and sent the sales of wireless sets through the roof.

A 1924 Atwater Kent breadboard radio

1921
Miss America

She stood only 5 feet 1 inch tall and weighed a mere 108 pounds. But 16-year-old Margaret Gorman of Washington, D.C. *(below, third from left)*, evidently had plenty of *something*. On September 7, Gorman was crowned the first Miss America in Atlantic City, New Jersey, beating out a handful of rival "beauty maids" from mid-Atlantic cities.

The contest was just one attraction in the two-day Fall Frolic dreamed up by local businessmen to keep tourists and their dollars in town past Labor Day. But it so captivated the public that by 1924 the Miss America pageant had stretched to five days, and the judges chose the winner from among 83 beauties from all across the country. A national institution had been born.

1922
Jazz Goes National

New Orleans—especially its red-light district, Storyville —was jumping to a totally new sound before World War I. Pioneered by black musicians like Jelly Roll Morton and King Oliver, jazz merged blues, Dixieland brass marching band music, ragtime, and folk styles and kept Louisiana toes tapping until 1917, when the hottest bands scattered after the navy shut down Storyville to keep sailors out of trouble.

King Oliver moved to Chicago, where his Creole Jazz Band set the mood for making whoopee at Prohibition-era speakeasies. In 1922 he invited a young New Orleans protégé, Louis Armstrong, to join him. At 22, Armstrong was already one of jazz's most inventive cornetists. His playing made him a darling of Chicago and earned him a stint with Fletcher Henderson, New York's foremost black bandleader. But by November 1925 he had come back to Chicago and into the studios of Okeh Records. His recordings would make him a household name and move jazz out of the speakeasies and into the mainstream.

Armstrong had his own group, the Hot Five, when he made his first hit record, "Heebie Jeebies," in 1926. Besides playing cornet, he was also the vocalist, giving many jazz fans their introduction to the nonsense syllables of scat singing.

1925
Science
on Trial

For fundamentalists, the barbarity of world war and the excesses of the Jazz Age were signs of nothing less than the moral collapse of Western society. At the root of the decline, they argued, lay Charles Darwin's theory of natural selection, which in their opinion denied any link between the divine and humankind and placed people squarely in the animal kingdom.

By 1925 antievolution feeling ran so hot that Tennessee made it a crime to teach anything but the biblical story of creation in public schools. High-school teacher John Scopes defied the law and was arrested, setting the stage for a trial that became a symbol of the clash between traditional religion and science.

Prominent defense attorney Clarence Darrow outargued the famed orator and three-time presidential candidate William Jennings Bryan, who assisted the prosecution, but the jury sided with Bryan. An appeals court later reversed Scopes's conviction on a technicality, and the tremendous publicity the trial received helped promote acceptance of Darwin's theory.

John Scopes (fifth from right) never testified at his own trial, the first to be broadcast live

on radio. Clarence Darrow (far left) and William Jennings Bryan stole the show.

1925
Frozen Food

Naturalist Clarence Birdseye made an important discovery while visiting fur trappers in eastern Canada between 1912 and 1917: Duck, caribou, and fish frozen in the bitter cold of midwinter had a better flavor and texture when cooked than those that had been frozen in the milder temperatures of fall and spring. Realizing that this must be connected to the speed  with which the carcasses were frozen, Birdseye returned to the United States and began eight years of experiments aimed at re-creating the process. By 1925 he had perfected a method that revolutionized the food industry. Put into practice at General Seafoods, his Massachusetts company, his quick-freeze system not only maintained a food's flavor, texture, and vitamin content but also delivered it in a rectangular package that simplified transport and storage and turned the Birds Eye brand into the first frozen convenience food.

1927
Lucky Lindy

Despite the heroics of the country's World War I aces and the triumph of Commander Richard Byrd, who flew over the North Pole in 1926, most Americans in 1927 associated airplanes with little more than barnstorming. Convinced of aviation's great potential, on May 20 Charles Lindbergh strapped himself into the wicker seat of a custom-built monoplane at Long Island's Roosevelt Field and at 7:52 a.m.

"Which way is Ireland?"

Charles Lindbergh, May 21, 1927

lifted off for Paris—3,610 miles and an ocean away. Alone, without a radio, and relying solely on dead reckoning, he slowed down once to ask an astonished fisherman for directions to Ireland but never stopped. After 33½ hours, Lindbergh landed at Le Bourget Aérodrome outside Paris. Lauded internationally for making the first nonstop solo flight across the Atlantic, he convinced millions that the age of transoceanic flight was near at hand.

A 1927 souvenir compass commemorating Lindbergh's flight

Charles Lindbergh stands beside the Spirit of St. Louis, named in honor of the St. Louis, Missouri, investors and aviation enthusiasts who financed the venture.

Photographed from another plane, Lindbergh's monoplane soars above Long Island shortly after takeoff. In the year following his flight, 14 pilots, three of them women, died trying to duplicate his feat. In 1928 Amelia Earhart succeeded, becoming the first woman to fly across the Atlantic.

1927
The First Talkie

Moviegoers were treated to a number of experiments with recorded sound in the '20s, but actors in feature films remained mute until *The Jazz Singer* debuted in New York's Warners' Theatre on October 6. Al Jolson's renditions of the songs "My Mammy" and "Toot, Toot, Tootsie" brought down the house, and his ad-libbed line "You ain't heard nothin' yet!" proved prophetic for the entire industry. Critics said talkies would turn cinema into bad theater, but most fans—including Walt Disney—knew better. The 26-year-old animator not only set his 1928 cartoon *Steamboat Willie* to music but used his own voice for the mischievous squeak of its button-eyed star, Mickey Mouse.

1929
The Great Crash

During the '20s almost everyone wanted a piece of the action in the stock market. Having raced from 66.24 in 1921 to 180.57 in 1925, the industrial average soared ever higher, reaching 469.49 on September 19, 1929. Some market analysts and economists warned that the bull market would stop raging soon, but millions of Americans continued speculating anyway.

Share prices were high, so many investors bought stock with money borrowed from their brokers. Called buying on margin, the practice permitted people to control investments whose value was as much as five or 10 times greater than what they could have swung using their own cash. These investors counted on rising prices to cover their loans when they sold stock. It was a bad bet: Prices slipped in early October. Brokers sent margin calls to their clients demanding payment of their loans. Many investors were forced to sell some or all of their stock because they didn't have the cash to repay their brokers. Such sales pushed prices even lower, causing still more losses and provoking new waves of margin calls. By the week of October 22 selling had reached panic pitch.

The industrial average, which had stood at 446.49 as recently as October 10, fell to 275.26 on Black Tuesday, October 29. In the following weeks more than a million people would lose $30 billion—an amount equal to almost a third of the year's gross national product. The collapse of the great Jazz Age bull market signaled a new and painful era—the Great Depression.

Crowds gather in front of the New York Stock Exchange on October 25, the day after panic selling turned the usually decorous exchange into a madhouse.

1931
A Towering Symbol

When the stock market crashed late in October 1929, workers were already tearing down the buildings on the site of the world's tallest skyscraper yet, the Empire State Building. Calling off the project would have incurred huge losses, so the builders forged ahead. On any given day the site swarmed with as many as 3,400 riveters, masons, electricians, and other workers, and in 14 months they had raised the skyscraper 102 stories and 1,250 feet high.

On May 1, President Hoover flipped a switch in Washington, turning on the lights. Although more than half the rentable space remained unoccupied because of the Depression, the tower was still a heartening symbol of American resolve during hard times. And even after it had been surpassed in height, the Empire State Building remained the world's most famous skyscraper, an American invention that changed the skyline of cities everywhere.

A steel man works on the Empire State Building in 1930. It replaced the Chrysler Building (near left) as the world's tallest skyscraper.

1932
The Great Depression

In a slow downward spiral, the Great Depression dragged Americans to the depths of misery and was nearing rock bottom by late 1932. Thousands of banks had failed, wiping out their depositors' savings. More than 13 million people—25 percent of the U.S. labor force—had lost their jobs, and wages had plunged to as little as a nickel an hour. A million or more impoverished vagabonds were wandering the country, including an estimated 200,000 children. Hunger drove the destitute to scavenge food for themselves and their families. "There is not a garbage dump in Chicago which is not diligently haunted by the hungry," literary critic Edmund Wilson observed.

President Herbert Hoover declared that charities and local governments should provide for impoverished Americans, and only in 1932 did he belatedly take measures to stimulate the economy. Unimpressed, voters gave Democratic candidate Franklin D. Roosevelt a landslide victory in the election that fall.

A jobless man peddles apples, an enterprise that frequently netted only a few cents a day. At right, a man waits in a bread line in San Francisco.

"I pledge you, I pledge myself, to a new deal for the American people. Let all of us here assembled constitute ourselves prophets of a new order of competence and courage."

Franklin D. Roosevelt, accepting the Democratic presidential nomination

One of the Depression era's numerous "Hoovervilles" huddles near the Seattle waterfront. Built by the down-and-out, these collections of shacks were named in mocking tribute to President Hoover, the frequent butt of jokes.

Around the World

1933
Hitler Comes to Power

"Like a blazing fire," proclaimed Radio Cologne on the night of January 29, 1933, "the news spreads across Germany; Adolf Hitler is chancellor of the Reich! A million hearts are aflame. Rejoicing and gratitude pour forth."

Defeated in war, mired in economic depression, humiliated by the Treaty of Versailles, and torn by political strife, Germany was ripe for Hitler's charismatic brand of leadership. A decorated World War I corporal, he and his National Socialist Party enjoyed wide support in all quarters of society, rich and poor.

Soon after becoming chancellor, Hitler abolished the democratic republic established after World War I, banned rival parties, and eliminated free speech. In spite of such dictatorial measures, Germans regained the faith in their country that the war had destroyed. With Hitler in power, one supporter recalled, "everyone felt that things would get better."

1933
FDR's First 100 Days

At his inauguration on March 4, 1933, Franklin D. Roosevelt set the tone that would define his first months in office. "This nation asks for action, and action now," he declared. "We must act and act quickly." True to his word, the new president proved more active during his first 100 days in office than many of his predecessors had been throughout their entire terms. His energy electrified the nation. "The whole country is with him," humorist Will Rogers said, "just so he does something."

In the hectic first three months of his "New Deal" domestic reform program, Roosevelt boosted morale by making the sale of beer and wine legal and passing 15 major bills, including the Emergency Banking Act and legislation designed to restore the faltering financial system. He also launched a host of recovery efforts, dubbed "alphabet soup" programs for the acronyms that identified them. The Civilian Conservation Corps (CCC) put 2.5 million young men to work on conservation and reforestation projects, and the Tennessee Valley Authority (TVA) brought hydroelectric power to rural southerners, and the Agricultural Adjustment Administration (AAA) gave aid to farmers.

The centerpiece of Roosevelt's New Deal was the National Industrial Recovery Act, which established the National Recovery Administration (NRA) as a way to get wages and prices under control and stimulate industrial growth. The NRA's Blue Eagle logo soon became a familiar sight on flags and badges at participating businesses. The act also set up the Public Works Administration (PWA), a $3.3-billion agency designed to create jobs by financing construction of schools, courthouses, and other municipal projects.

While critics denounced such programs as creeping socialism or even Communism, most Americans supported Roosevelt's decisive actions. Interior Secretary Harold Ickes summed up the prevailing mood: "It's more than a New Deal," he said. "It's a new world."

Roosevelt greets admirers in Warm Springs, Georgia. Soon after his inauguration a supporter wrote him declaring, "People are looking to you almost as they look to God."

"When these winds hit us, we and our misery were suddenly covered with dust. . . . If the wind blew one way, here came the dark dust from Oklahoma. Another way and it was the gray dust from Kansas. Still another way, the brown dust from Colorado and New Mexico."

A Texas farmer, 1934

1933
The Dust Bowl

Decades of careless plowing and overgrazing that stripped the Great Plains of its natural mantle of deep-rooted prairie grass set the scene for the worst agricultural disaster in American history. In 1932, a prolonged drought set in. The exposed soil grew steadily drier and more vulnerable to erosion, and in 1933 residents watched worriedly as fall winds churned up clouds of dust. The following spring was worse. Winds of up to 60 miles an hour howled across the prairie, and the powdery soil rose two miles into the sky, burying livestock, blanketing houses, and filling mouths and lungs. In May a two-day-long "black blizzard" scooped up 300 million tons of soil and carried it all the way to East Coast cities including Washington, D.C., where the air was so thick with fine silt that the streetlights were on at midday.

The worst-hit parts of Colorado, Kansas, Oklahoma, Texas, and New Mexico—150 million square miles in all—became known as the Dust Bowl, and life there was misery. Wrote one Oklahoma woman, "We dream of the faint gurgling sound of dry soil sucking in the grateful moisture. . . . But we wake to another day of wind and dust and hopes deferred. . . ." At President Roosevelt's behest, agents of the Department of Agriculture's Soil Conservation Service traveled the plains introducing farmers to proper plowing and cultivating practices, and the Civilian Conservation Corps began planting millions of trees to serve as windbreaks. But money couldn't buy rain.

It would be six years before the drought broke. By then, hundreds of thousands of people had left the plains for greener pastures. In one 15-month period alone, 86,000 refugees from the Dust Bowl headed west on U.S. Highway 66, crossing the California border at Yuma, Arizona, with hopes for a new start.

An Oklahoma family (below) pauses on their journey west to find work, their car loaded with a mattress, stove, stovepipes, and other household essentials. More than 750,000 people displaced by the drought resettled in California and the Pacific Northwest in one of the largest internal migrations in U.S. history.

1934 Hoover's G-Men

Melvin H. Purvis (below, left), head of the Bureau of Investigation's Chicago field office, gets a congratulatory handshake from Hoover for the operation in which John Dillinger was killed outside a Chicago movie theater on July 22.

Criminals whose activities violated federal law or spilled across state lines found a formidable foe in Director J. Edgar Hoover's Bureau of Investigation. In 1934, Congress gave his agents the right to carry guns and make arrests as well as investigate crimes; a year later the word "Federal" was added to the bureau's name.

In an effort to recruit a crime-fighting force of the highest caliber possible, Director Hoover decreed that only law-school graduates, certified public accountants, and seasoned police officers could apply to be agents. Once chosen, they had to prove their mettle in a three-month training program covering topics such as criminal psychology, fingerprinting, and ballistics.

When on the trail of such criminals as the notorious bank robber John Dillinger, Hoover directed his elite cadre of government men— G-men, for short—to "act first, talk afterward" and to "shoot straight and get the right man."

Junior G-man badge

JUNIOR G-MAN

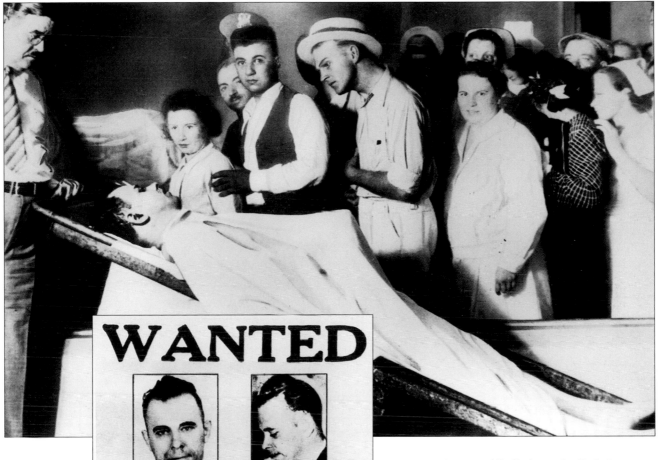

WANTED

JOHN HERBERT DILLINGER

On June 23, 1934, HOMER S. CUMMINGS, Attorney General of the United States, under the authority vested in him by an Act of Congress approved June 6, 1934, offered a reward of

$10,000.00

for the capture of John Herbert Dillinger or a reward of

$5,000.00

for information leading to the arrest of John Herbert Dillinger.

DESCRIPTION

Age, 32 years; Height, 5 feet 7-1/8 inches; Weight, 153 pounds; Build, medium; Hair, medium chestnut; Eyes, grey; Complexion, medium; Occupation, machinist; Marks and scars, 1/2 inch scar back left hand, scar middle upper lip, brown mole between eyebrows.

All claims to any of the aforesaid rewards and all questions and disputes that may arise as among claimants to the foregoing rewards shall be passed upon by the Attorney General and his decisions shall be final and conclusive. The right is reserved to divide and allocate portions of any of said rewards as between several claimants. No part of the aforesaid rewards shall be paid to any official or employee of the Department of Justice.

If you are in possession of any information concerning the whereabouts of John Herbert Dillinger, communicate immediately by telephone or telegraph collect to the nearest office of the Division of Investigation, United States Department of Justice, the local addresses of which are set forth on the reverse side of this notice.

JOHN EDGAR HOOVER, DIRECTOR,
DIVISION OF INVESTIGATION,
UNITED STATES DEPARTMENT OF JUSTICE,
WASHINGTON, D. C.

June 23, 1934

Put on public display at the Cook County morgue, John Dillinger's corpse was propped up so that the people filing past could get a better look at it (above). His numerous robberies and daring jailbreaks had gained him nationwide notoriety, and news broadcasts about the ambush of Dillinger drew thousands of people to the site where he died.

At the time that the wanted poster at left was being circulated, John Dillinger had been named Public Enemy Number One by Hoover. Dillinger's successor as top man on the enemies list was bank robber Charles "Pretty Boy" Floyd. After his capture, Lester Gillis, alias "Baby Face" Nelson, a confederate of Dillinger, rose to the top.

1935
Social Security

A cornerstone of President Roosevelt's New Deal was the Social Security Act. One of the most sweeping laws in American history, it insured 26 million American workers against income loss from unemployment, old age, and blindness. The average salary at the time was less than $1,200, and workers were hard pressed to save enough to live decently after retirement. The guarantee of a pension, funded jointly by employers and employees, relieved the many Americans fearful of financial hardship in their later years.

Social Security poster

The monthly benefit initially ranged from $10 to $85—modest amounts even then—and remained frozen at those levels until 1950. The first person to start receiving a Social Security check was a woman named Ida Fuller, who paid in a total of about $24 in payroll taxes before retiring, lived into her nineties, and eventually collected more than $20,000.

1937
A Triumph for Labor

For its first 13 days the sit-down strike by the fledgling United Auto Workers that idled the General Motors' Fisher Body plant in Flint, Michigan, was peaceful, if tense. But on January 11, the tension escalated into an armed clash. Determined to drive the strikers out, managers summoned the Flint police, who arrived in riot gear, broke windows, and fired tear-gas grenades and buckshot into the plant. The strikers answered with a hail of bricks, steel hinges, and bottles, and for the next month they held their ground.

During that time the strike spread from Flint to the rest of GM's 14-state empire, halting production. Facing losses of a million dollars a day, GM caved in on February 11, signing a contract that gave the UAW unprecedented bargaining power. It was a monumental triumph for American labor. "Even if we got not one damn thing out of it other than that," recalled one striker, "we at least had a right to open our mouths without fear." Soon after the contract was signed, the Supreme Court greatly strengthened labor's hand: It upheld the constitutionality of the Wagner Act of 1935, a landmark law that empowered employees to bargain collectively and to join unions.

Strike fever swept the country, and workers rushed to join what *Fortune* magazine called "one of the greatest mass movements in our history." That movement was at times a bloody endeavor. Three months after the Flint victory, police in Chicago used gunfire to break up a rally of 1,500 Republic Steel employees and their families, killing 10 and wounding more than 100. In industry after industry, the struggles of 1937 shifted the balance of power between employer and employee, and unions became a political, social, and economic force that changed the fortunes of the individual worker and the nation itself.

A policeman clubs a striker during a rally near the Republic Steel factory in Chicago. What began as "a family picnic sort of thing," as one observer described it, went down in history as the Memorial Day Massacre.

Around the World

1937
Japan Makes War on China

What has been called the first battle of World War II was fought by Japanese and Chinese soldiers west of Peking on July 7. Begun as a skirmish, the clash quickly turned into full-scale war when the Japanese seized Peking and then moved on other cities.

On August 28, Japanese planes bombed Shanghai's railway station, where 1,800 citizens, most of them women and children, were waiting for an overdue train to flee the city. Only 300 survived the devastation. Hearst Metrotone newsreel photographer H. S. Wong filmed the raid, capturing the scene above. "It was a horrible sight," he recalled. "Dead and injured lay strewn across the tracks and platform. Limbs lay all over the place."

Despite a heroic resistance at Shanghai in which as many as 250,000 defenders died, the port city fell in October. From Shanghai the Japanese marched on to the city of Nanking, where they implemented one of the most sadistic campaigns in modern warfare; among the victims were as many as 20,000 women and girls who were raped and murdered. But it was Wong's picture of the motherless baby in Shanghai, reproduced in countless magazines and newspapers, that gave Americans their first look at a war that would draw their nation in four years down the road.

1939
Gone With the Wind

> "Frankly, my dear, I don't give a damn."

Rhett Butler

The Hollywood movie industry hit its peak in the 1930s, and 1939's *Gone With the Wind* represented the nation's dream factory at its extravagant and star-studded best. The romanticized rendering of the Civil War mesmerized moviegoers, just as *The Birth of a Nation* had a generation earlier *(pages 56-57)*. Depression-weary viewers identified with Scarlett O'Hara, the steely, spirited belle who endures loss of fortune and near-starvation but declares that "tomorrow is another day." A scornful remark that hero Rhett Butler flings at Scarlett—"Frankly, my dear, I don't give a damn"—shocked audiences. Never before had they heard profanity in a Hollywood movie, and the line became a fixture in American lingo.

Dashing Rhett Butler, played by Clark Gable, scandalizes a charity ball by asking war widow Scarlett O'Hara (Vivien Leigh), still dressed in mourning black, to join him in leading the Virginia reel. Produced by David O. Selznick, the movie took three years to make. At almost $4 million, it was Hollywood's costliest to date.

Around the World

1939
Hitler Invades Poland

Having looked the other way as Adolf Hitler's resurgent Germany annexed Austria and the Sudetenland in western Czechoslovakia in 1938, Europe's leaders hoped that Hitler's appetite for land had finally been sated. But early on Friday, September 1, 1939—nine days after signing a nonaggression pact with the Soviet Union—the Führer revealed just how hungry he still was.

In the predawn darkness, without a declaration of war and on false claims that Poland had attacked German territory, Hitler's forces invaded Poland by land, sea, and air. The first shots were fired in Danzig, the Baltic port that separated East Prussia from the rest of the Reich; before day's end Germany had annexed the city.

World War II officially began two days later, on September 3, when both Britain and France declared war on Germany. The

Londoners (above) react with dismay to the news that Hitler's SS troops (right) have invaded the port of Danzig in northern Poland. It would take Hitler just over a month to claim victory.

British bombed ships in the northern German city of Kiel and rained propaganda leaflets over the Rhineland while the French raided Germany's western border, but political and military unpreparedness prevented the Allies from offering Poland more substantial aid. Outmanned and lacking modern equipment, the Poles were unable to stop 1.5 million German troops and 1,700 tanks from pummeling Cracow, Warsaw, and other Polish cities. When the Red Army crossed the border into eastern Poland on September 17, the country's grave situation became hopeless.

The world watched in horror as Poland disappeared from the map, carved up by Hitler and Joseph Stalin. "This is terribly wrong," wrote an American correspondent. "We've only had 21 years of peace following the war that was supposed to be the last war. It looks like certain danger on the horizon."

A twin-engine Heinkel, one of the more than 1,500 German aircraft mobilized to invade Poland, rains bombs on Warsaw. The city fiercely resisted air and artillery bombardment for 26 days before capitulating.

1941
Pearl Harbor

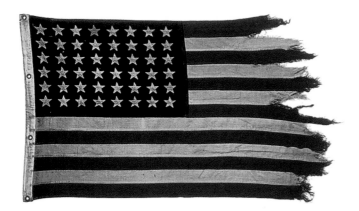

When Japan joined Germany and Italy as a partner in the military Axis in 1940, relations with the U.S. took a downward turn, then worsened further after Japan occupied French Indochina in 1941. U.S. military planners thought that Japan might attempt a surprise attack on Pearl Harbor, the home port of the Pacific Fleet in Hawaii. Yet when 183 Japanese planes swept toward the harbor on the morning of December 7, the surprise was total; they encountered no effective air patrol or antiaircraft fire. Their primary targets—eight battleships, nine cruisers, 29 destroyers, and 39 other warships—were anchored beam to beam and bow to bow, and planes were lined up wing tip to wing tip at neighboring airfields.

The effect of the bombs and torpedoes was devastating. Most of the planes on Oahu were wrecked, and 18 ships, including all the battleships, were sunk or disabled. The harbor was in chaos. "I went to hell and back I can't tell you how many times that day," said an army nurse. "We all did." Stateside, news flashes interrupting afternoon radio shows alerted Americans to the Pearl Harbor disaster. Isolationist sentiment vanished, and the nation united to face the bitter task that suddenly lay ahead.

The bombed and torpedoed Arizona (right) begins to sink, taking 1,177 crewmen down with her. The flag of the California (above) survived the attack.

1941
War!

So great was the shock and out-rage following Japan's attack on Pearl Harbor on December 7 that every vestige of more than 20 years of American isolationism evapo-rated in an instant. "The indecision was over," recalled Secretary of War Henry Stimson. "A crisis had come in a way which would unite our people."

Eight in 10 Americans opposed a declaration of war before the raid, polls showed. But on December 8, when President Franklin Roosevelt (*above*) asked a joint session of Con-gress to declare war on Japan, only one of the assembled representatives voted no. Four days later, Roosevelt would ask them to recognize a state of war again, this time with Germany and Italy, Japan's Axis partners, who de-clared war on the United States on De-cember 11. The vote was unanimous.

1942
Americans Behind Barbed Wire

Japanese Americans bore the brunt of the nation's initial rage over Pearl Harbor. Within days of the attack, government au-thorities had searched Japanese homes, shuttered Japanese banks, stores, and newspapers, and taken into custody more than a thousand Japanese community leaders. First Lady Eleanor Roosevelt pleaded for restraint, writing in a newspaper column that loyal resi-

dents of Japanese extraction "must not feel they have suddenly ceased to be Americans." But by February of 1942 fears about Japanese "spies, saboteurs and 5th columnists" were so pervasive that the president authorized the forced removal of all persons of Japanese descent, American-born citizens as well as resident aliens, from designated military areas.

When much of western California, Oregon, and Washington was declared a military area the following month, about 120,000 Japanese Americans were told to report to assembly centers. From there they were transported by train to internment camps in eastern California, Arizona, and five other states. None of the internees had been convicted of a crime. Yet the majority were kept behind barbed wire and under guard until 1944—a gross injustice for which the federal government in 1990 started paying $1.25 billion in reparations.

A man and his grandsons await an evacuation bus in California in May 1942. Almost two-thirds of the internees, including the owner of the Oakland store at left, were U.S. citizens.

1942
The Battle
of Midway

On June 4, six months after the U.S. Pacific Fleet was mauled at Pearl Harbor, over 100 Japanese ships were nearing Midway, a tiny atoll at the northwest tip of the Hawaiian Islands that was a valuable midocean fueling station for the U.S. The armada included four carriers with 261 aircraft, hallmarks of a new type of naval warfare that was fought largely with planes rather than armed ships. Although Midway would be an asset to Japan, the offensive's principal goal was to destroy what remained of the U.S. fleet.

Unknown to the Japanese, American cryptographers had broken their secret code and intercepted messages about their battle plan. With that information, the outnumbered Americans were able to sink the armada's four carriers, and all its aircraft went down as well; the U.S. fleet lost only one of its three carriers. Along with dealing a disastrous blow to the Japanese navy, the furious American defense stopped the enemy's push west. With the victory at Midway, the tide began to turn in the Pacific war.

Eisenhower reviews U.S. troops on the eve of the D-Day invasion. When one soldier saw the concern on Eisenhower's face, he called out, "Now quit worrying, General, we'll take care of this thing for you."

1944
D-Day in Normandy

"We are about to embark upon the Great Crusade, toward which we have striven these many months. The eyes of the world are upon you. The hopes and prayers of liberty-loving people everywhere march with you."

Eisenhower's order of the day for June 6 to the Allied Expeditionary Force

By late spring 1944 American and British bombers had been wreaking havoc on German targets for almost two years. Significant victories had been won. Allied troops had advanced halfway up the boot of Italy and liberated Rome. Far to the east, the Soviet Red Army, after four years of horrendous combat, was pushing back the massive German invasion that had begun in 1941. But France, Belgium, and the other occupied countries of western Europe were still under Nazi rule. Their best hope for freedom, and the Allies' best chance for winning the war, lay in an invasion of France. If successful, it would force Germany's already overextended armies to defend their hold on western Europe at the same time that they were fighting furiously in the Soviet Union.

Adolf Hitler so feared fighting a two-front war that he ordered the entire French coastline fortified with artillery emplacements, concrete and steel bunkers, and beach barriers. Duped by an Allied campaign of deception into believing the invasion would take place at Calais in northern France, where the English Channel is narrowest, he had his Atlantic Wall made especially strong near Calais.

But when June 6, D-Day, finally dawned, the Allies came ashore not at Calais but in Normandy, over a hundred miles to the southwest. German defenders still inflicted heavy casualties—especially at the four-mile-long, cliff-lined beach the Allies called Omaha—but by nightfall the gravity of Hitler's misjudgment was clear. More than 150,000 Allied soldiers, 57,000 of them American, had pierced the Atlantic Wall and opened the western front. Hundreds of thousands more troops, waiting offshore and in England, would join the offensive in the days to come. Under the command of General Dwight D. Eisenhower, they would liberate Paris 11 weeks later.

American troops load landing ships at Brixham, south of Exeter on England's southern coast, on May 27, 10 days before D-Day.

1944
Battle of
the Bulge

Eisenhower's armies rode a tide of optimism after liberating Paris on August 25. Surging east toward Germany and north into Belgium on the heels of the enemy, by mid-September the Allies commanded a line extending from the North Sea through Belgium and down to Switzerland. But as they neared Germany's western frontier, the enemy's resolve stiffened, slowing the Allied advance.

German forces had been observed massing across the border from Belgium's mountainous Ardennes region, but the Allies assumed that they were preparing for a defense of the fatherland, not for an offensive. So when the Germans counterattacked on December 16, they surprised the Allies completely and caused a bulge in the Allied line that gave the ensuing battle its name.

Finally stopped 60 miles into Belgium and nearly encircled by General Patton's Third Army, the Germans suffered huge casualties and lost almost all their tanks and aircraft. Their attack was Adolf Hitler's last in northwest Europe, and their retreat was the beginning of the end for Nazi Germany.

American soldiers (left) emerge from a dense fog and run past a shell-shattered building in a Belgian town during the Battle of the Bulge. Heavy snow, bitter cold, and a lack of supplies compounded the troops' misery. Like the rifleman below, many had to improvise ways to stay warm.

1945
The Yalta Conference

British prime minister Winston Churchill, President Franklin Roosevelt, and Soviet premier Joseph Stalin *(inset, left to right)* had been allies for four years when they gathered at the Black Sea resort of Yalta in February, but Britain and the United States had never collaborated with the U.S.S.R. on military operations. United against Germany but divided by hostile political systems, the two Western leaders on the one hand and Stalin on the other made suspicious bedfellows from the first. Now, as the three men sat down to plot the shape of the postwar world, Germany teetered on the brink of collapse, western Europe lay in ruins, and Communist forces controlled much of eastern Europe, including Poland. Permanent Communist rule of eastern Europe was abhorrent to Washington and London. Yet Roosevelt desperately wanted the Red Army to join in the fighting against Japan, so he and Churchill were anxious not to offend Stalin.

In a series of trade-offs, the Western leaders agreed to recognize Poland's Soviet-installed government in return for Stalin's promise of free elections there. In addition, Stalin committed himself to declaring war on Japan in exchange for a guarantee that Russian territory lost to Japan in two earlier wars would be returned. Observers initially hailed the Yalta agreements as a "landmark in human history." But when Stalin reneged on his promise of free elections, any good feeling generated by the agreements vanished. The word "Yalta" entered the American lexicon not as the keystone of world peace but as a synonym for the betrayal of Poland and the birthplace of the Cold War.

1945
Victory on
Iwo Jima

On February 19, marines
landed on Iwo Jima, an
eight-square-mile island
1,000 miles southeast of Tokyo. To the
Japanese, it was "the doorkeeper to
the Imperial capital," to be defended
at any cost. From an American point
of view, Iwo Jima was critical as a base
for fighter planes and as an emergency
landing site for B-29 Superfortress
bombers flying between the Mariana
Islands and Japan. Wrested from the
enemy in 1944, the Marianas brought
Japan within the giant bomber's 1,600-
mile range for the first time, but the
distance was often too great for a crip-
pled plane to make it back.

Iwo Jima was riddled with tunnels
and caves in which the enemy hid, and
it took nearly a month of bloody fighting, sometimes hand-to-hand, to take
the island. More than 6,000 Americans
were dead and another 18,000 were
wounded, but Iwo Jima was salvation
for the B-29 crews who made 2,400
emergency landings there by war's
end. One pilot said, "Whenever I land
on this island, I thank God for the
men who fought for it."

*Under intense fire after storm-
ing Iwo Jima on February 19,
U.S. Marines crawl up a slope
leading off the landing beach.
The large number of casualties
made the operation the costli-
est in Marine Corps history.*

Around the World

1945
The Holocaust

Of all the groups the Nazis considered enemies of the state, they despised Jews the most. Blamed for Germany's humiliation during World War I and for its economic woes afterward, they became targets of harassment as soon as Adolf Hitler was named chancellor.

About half of the country's half-million Jews fled persecution between 1933 and 1939, as did two-thirds of Austria's 180,000 Jews. But for the nine million Jews of central and eastern Europe there was little chance for escape. When their nations fell in 1939, they became the chief victims of the Nazis' attempt to destroy the Jews completely.

Thousands died of starvation, exposure, and disease in labor camps and ghettos, and thousands more were shot by execution squads following the 1941 invasion of Russia. Then, after the Germans agreed in 1942 on what they called a "final solution of the Jewish question," still more Jews were shipped by train to special camps in Poland. There the able-bodied were issued prison stripes and made to work while all others— the sick and the aged, the children, and most women—were stripped naked, shaved bald, and killed with poison gas. Some six million Jews—more than one-third of world Jewry— perished in this way.

When American troops liberated Buchenwald, a camp in central Germany, in April 1945, they found the story of the Holocaust written on the faces of some 20,000 slave laborers who had survived (right). They also found there and at other camps lifeless bodies "dumped like garbage rotting in the sun." Writer Martha Gellhorn accompanied American troops and witnessed such scenes. "There can never be peace if there is cruelty like this in the world," she wrote. "And if ever again we tolerate such cruelty we have no right to peace."

1945
Hiroshima

When Harry Truman became president following Franklin Roosevelt's death on April 12, Germany's surrender was just weeks away, but in the Pacific, war raged on. Twelve days before, American troops had landed on the island of Okinawa, just 350 miles from Japan, and they were dying by the thousands in combat as ferocious as they had endured on Iwo Jima *(pages 106-107)*. The loss of Iwo Jima had not sapped the Japanese military's fanatical will to fight, nor had the American bombs that were devastating Japan's war industries and incinerating vast tracts of its cities.

Truman was determined to end the war, but with no sign that Japan was contemplating surrender, he gave his approval to a plan for an invasion, scheduled for November. However, the president hoped for an alternative that would spare American lives; he dreaded the prospect of "an Okinawa from one end of Japan to the other." That alternative presented itself on July 16, when the first nuclear bomb developed by the government's top-secret Manhattan Project was successfully tested. Truman made his decision: The United States would, if necessary, use what he called "the most terrible bomb in the history of the world." Ten days later, the United States and its allies Britain and China demanded that Japan surrender or face "prompt and utter destruction." Japan rejected the ultimatum, and Truman gave the order to use the new weapon.

The world entered the nuclear age on August 6, when a single atomic bomb was detonated over the city of Hiroshima, flattening it instantaneously. A second bomb was dropped on Nagasaki three days later, and on August 14 Japan surrendered.

A mushroom cloud rises over Hiroshima after the explosion of the atomic bomb on August 6. Eighty thousand civilians were killed instantly. Among the dead was the owner of this wristwatch, whose hands stopped at the moment of the blast.

The roofless, windowless shells of reinforced-concrete buildings remain standing amid the flattened remains of Hiroshima after the bombing.

1946
ENIAC

The world's first digital computer was unveiled in February *(above)* at the University of Pennsylvania, where it had been developed by engineer Presper Eckert and physicist John Mauchly to calculate trajectories for artillery shells and bombs and compute ballistics tables for the army. Completed too late to help in the war effort, ENIAC (Electronic Numerical Integrator and Computer) weighed a hulking 30 tons and occupied 1,800 square feet. It was programmed by means of hundreds of cables and several thousand switches and dials and performed its calculations using 17,468 vacuum tubes that made it hundreds of times faster than earlier electromechanical devices. Mauchly and Eckert's other great triumph was UNIVAC, a business computer that helped usher in the peacetime computer age.

Above, Jackie Robinson signs an autograph during spring training in the Dominican

1947 Breaking Barriers

When Jackie Robinson stepped up to the plate in a Brooklyn Dodgers uniform on April 15, the former Negro Leagues star ended one of America's most visible forms of segregation—the racial division of professional baseball. Although popular with many fans, the first baseman was the recipient of

> "I'm not concerned with your liking or disliking me. . . . All I ask is that you respect me as a human being."
>
> Jackie Robinson, 1955

taunts and hate mail. Some of the players were hostile, too; in the first season alone, Robinson was struck by pitched balls nine times. Through it all, he stayed focused on the game, winning Rookie of the Year and later a place in the Baseball Hall of Fame.

Republic in 1948. At home, he received death threats (inset) as well as admiration.

1947
Baby Boom!

Americans started having more babies in 1942, reversing a long downturn in birthrates as World War II brought the Great Depression to an end. But with so many men away from home, it was not until the postwar years that the birthrate skyrocketed, reaching a high of 26.6 newborns per 1,000 Americans in 1947. To the surprise of demographers—and just about everybody else—the boom kept going for another 17 years, as unprecedented prosperity made it possible for even very young couples to marry and start families. The result was a huge demand for baby-related goods ranging from toys to pediatrician Benjamin Spock's 1946 childcare guide *(above)*. The biggest purchase of all was a home for the new family, more likely than not a house in the new suburbs that were spreading across the land *(right)*.

Built primarily for young families, the Long Island suburb of farmland; prices started at $8,000 a house. Truck supervisor

Levittown, shown here in about 1950, packed 17,400 homes onto 4,000 acres of former
Bernard Levey and family (left) moved into one of Levittown's Cape Cod models in 1948.

1948
The Facts
About Sex

In 1948, an 804-page book from a medical publishing house became a runaway bestseller. *Sexual Behavior in the Human Male,* by Indiana University professor Alfred Kinsey, was packed with statistics based on interviews with 5,300 white men. For Americans of the day, the numbers were shocking: Kinsey reported, for example, that 85 percent of men had had premarital sex, one in three had had at least one homosexual experience, and as many as 45 percent of married men had had affairs. Although denounced by some commentators, the "Kinsey Report" got a warm reception from most Americans for shedding light on topics that had long been taboo. Its eagerly awaited sequel, *Sexual Behavior in the Human Female,* put Kinsey on the cover of *Time* in 1953. Although critics have pointed out serious flaws in Kinsey's methods, few have questioned the great impact the two books had on relaxing American views of sex.

1948
The Berlin Airlift

After the war, Joseph Stalin tightened his grip on Soviet-occupied East Germany and the rest of eastern Europe. Determined to choke off Western influence behind his Iron Curtain, he refused to let the East take part in the Marshall Plan, proposed by Secretary of State George Marshall *(inset, above)* in 1947 to revive Europe's devastated economies.

The next year saw the first crisis of the Cold War. When Stalin learned that the United States, Britain, and France were moving toward independence for the portion of Germany they occupied, he reacted by blockading land and water routes to Berlin. Located deep in East Germany, the city was, in accord with the Yalta agreements *(page 105)*, administered by the Soviet Union and the three Western allies.

Contrary to Stalin's aim, the allies did not abandon Berlin. Instead, the United States and Britain mounted a mammoth airlift to supply the city. On May 12, 1949, having failed to dislodge the Western allies or stop Germany's rebirth as a democracy in the West, Stalin lifted the blockade.

Berliners watch an American plane carrying food and supplies come in for a landing at Tempelhof Airfield. During the 11-month blockade British and American transports landed around the clock, often at intervals of four minutes or less.

Around the World

1949
China Goes Communist

The United States spent almost $3 billion after World War II to shore up China's Nationalist government and its leader, Chiang Kai-shek. Though his regime was corrupt, Chiang seemed the best hope of maintaining a bulwark against Communist expansion in Asia.

Since the 1920s, when a fragmented China was ruled by despotic regional warlords, Chiang and his Communist rivals had alternated between uneasy alliance and all-out conflict. They joined forces to seize power from the warlords in 1927, then took arms against each other in a vicious civil war that continued through 1937. When Japan invaded China that year, the Nationalists and the Communists called a truce that endured to the end of World War II. The civil war resumed, but with a decisive shift in power. Communist leader Mao Zedong had spent the years of truce building up his forces, and they now dealt the Nationalists one defeat after another. Steadily losing support among the people, in 1949 Chiang retreated to the island of Formosa, now Taiwan, where he reestablished his government. On October 1, Mao proudly declared mainland China a Communist state.

1950
Charge It, Please

Salesman Frank McNamara was entertaining clients at a New York City restaurant when he discovered he hadn't brought enough cash. The embarrassment gave McNamara an idea. Brainstorming with his friend Ralph Schneider, an attorney, he came up with the Diners Club, a credit card for use at restaurants and hotels. Although some businesses provided charge cards for their own customers, this would be the first card accepted by multiple firms. Introduced on a small scale on February 28, 1950, Diners Club grew quickly: The next year, 42,000 cardholders charged more than a million dollars. In 1952 department-store heir Alfred Bloomingdale bankrolled still rapider expansion, and America's love affair with the credit card was under way. Marveled *Time* magazine in 1958, "The credit card has risen as a new symbol of status that enables one to rent a plane or boat or car, give parties in nightclubs, even go on a full-blown safari in Africa without putting down a penny."

1950
War in Korea

American soldiers wrap themselves in sleeping bags in a vain attempt to get warm during the retreat of late 1950.

> "Those who did not build a fire were sometimes found frozen to death. . . . Those who did . . . were sometimes found shot to death beside . . . their fire."

American soldier describing the 1950 retreat

At the end of World War II, the Allies split the former Japanese colony of Korea along the 38th parallel, with the North administered by the Soviet Union and the South by the United States. Over the next few years the Soviets and the Americans gradually withdrew their forces, and the two Koreas were all but forgotten as the world focused on Germany, Eastern Europe, and China's civil war and revolution *(page 117)*.

On June 25, 1950, South Korea and the United States were caught completely off guard when 90,000 North Korean troops began pouring across the border. Dead set against any Communist expansion, President Truman rallied the United Nations Security Council to approve a multinational defense force. Commanded by General Douglas MacArthur, it took a terrible beating at first, but in September he launched an audacious attack behind enemy lines, near the 38th parallel. The North Koreans fled back across the border, with U.N. troops close behind. By late November they had advanced deep into North Korea and were within striking distance of neighboring Communist China. Confident of victory, MacArthur dismissed Chinese rumblings about intervening in the conflict. But on November 25, 300,000 Chinese troops crossed into North Korea. In ferocious fighting amid subzero temperatures, the U.N. soldiers retreated to the 38th parallel.

There the two sides faced off for two years. A cease-fire was finally concluded in 1953. After three years of war that killed about 600,000 soldiers on both sides and as many as two million civilians, a new border was established in roughly the same place as before. The tensions between the two Koreas would outlast the Cold War, and in the 1990s, the border was the most heavily fortified in the world.

U.S. troops sprint past a dead North Korean soldier without a second glance in September 1950. By the next year, both sides were dug in along a static front.

1952
Witch Hunt

In February 1950, Wisconsin's Senator Joseph McCarthy made headlines with what he claimed was a list of 205 Communists in the government. The list turned out to be nothing of the kind, but by then it didn't matter; Joe McCarthy was riding high, accusing both prominent and obscure Americans of disloyalty, smearing those who challenged him, frightening timorous politicians into silence, and destroying reputations and careers. Cheered at the 1952 Republican convention, McCarthy got his own congressional committee that fall, giving him a chance to badger government officials at hearings that were more like inquisitions. By 1954, the public had had enough. Falling as fast as he had risen, McCarthy was condemned by the Senate that December. He died three years later from the effects of heavy drinking.

1954
Television Takes Center Stage

Engineers had been working with experimental television sets since the 1920s, but it was not until the boom years after World War II that television became a fixture in the American home. As advertisers and sponsors shifted to the new medium, radio shows popular for a decade or more went off the air. In 1954, television's gross revenues—$593 million—finally surpassed radio's earnings. By then many radio performers had made the leap to television, including Jack Benny, Lucille Ball, and the Nelson family (right). There were also plenty of new television celebrities, such as endearingly awkward variety-show host Ed Sullivan (below), whom rival Fred Allen once said would "stay on television as long as other people have talent." Television became so popular that radio was not the only victim of its success; movie theaters and even magazines also lost money.

Four farm children with their canine companion enjoy Ed Sullivan's Toast of the Town variety show, a Sunday-night institution on CBS from 1948 until 1971.

The Adventures of Ozzie and Harriet starred "America's favorite family," the real-life Nelsons—father, mother, and their two sons, David (left) and Ricky (right), shown in matching shirts below. Ozzie Nelson, a former bandleader, wrote the scripts for the popular series, which aired from 1952 to 1966.

1954 Attack on Polio

Polio was once America's summer scourge. When an epidemic hit, swimming pools and movie theaters closed to curb the contagion's spread, yet tens of thousands still came down with polio. Most recovered; others died or were left paralyzed. In 1954, researcher Jonas Salk *(below)* put a new vaccine to the test with a trial involving 650,000 first, second, and third graders in 44 states; parents feared polio so much that the vast majority consented to their chil

dren's participation. The result was a decisive victory for Salk's vaccine. United States polio cases dropped from 38,694 in 1954 to 5,787 three years later; by 1961, when an oral vaccine was introduced, the summer scourge was almost gone.

1954 Brown v. the Board of Education

Linda Brown stands ready to attend New Summer, the white elementary school near her home. Before the Supreme Court handed down its decision, she had to cross a dangerous railway switchyard to catch the bus to an all-black school.

Guided by Chief Justice Earl Warren (center), the Warren Court made a number of land-mark decisions.

Although there was an elementary school just four blocks from the Topeka, Kansas, home of Oliver Brown and his family, his eight-year-old daughter, Linda, wasn't allowed to enroll there. Because she was black, she had to travel by bus to a school 25 blocks away. When Oliver Brown's request to have Linda transferred to the nearby school was denied, he sued the board of education. In 1952 the case came before the Supreme Court, which grouped it with four other school-desegregation cases; the key attorney on the desegregation side was NAACP counsel Thurgood Marshall. The decision would affect 12 million children attending segregated schools in 21 states.

Chief Justice Earl Warren announced the Court's unanimous opinion on May 17, 1954: "We conclude that in the field of public education the doctrine of 'separate but equal' has no place. Separate educational facilities are inherently unequal." It was "the sweetest of days," NAACP leader Roy Wilkins later recalled.

> "... the doctrine of 'separate but equal' has no place."
>
> Chief Justice Earl Warren, 1954

1955
The Montgomery Bus Boycott

On December 1, a black seamstress named Rosa Parks *(inset)* boarded a bus in Montgomery, Alabama, and took a seat in the middle of the bus, behind the whites-only section. A few stops later, the driver told Parks to give her seat to a white passenger and move farther back. When she refused, she was arrested. Local black activists announced a one-day bus boycott, then decided to keep it going to achieve improvements for black passengers, such as abolishing the requirement that they surrender their seat to whites on crowded buses. The boycott committee's leader, Martin Luther King Jr., thought an agreement could be reached within a few days. However, the city administration and the bus company refused to budge, and the boycott stretched into months. With the *Brown* decision *(opposite)* as an encouraging precedent, the committee filed suit seeking complete desegregation of the buses. The case made its way to the Supreme Court, which on November 13, 1956, declared Alabama's bus-segregation laws unconstitutional. It was another giant stride toward equality for black Americans.

> "... we are determined here in Montgomery to work and fight until justice runs down like water and righteousness like a mighty stream."
>
> The Reverend Martin Luther King Jr., December 5, 1955

1955
Faster
Food

Chicago milk-shake-machine salesman Ray Kroc's best customer by far was a drive-in in California—instead of the usual one or two machines, McDonald's had bought 10. His curiosity piqued, Kroc traveled to California in 1954 and discovered that the McDonald brothers had created a marvel of efficiency: an assembly-line-style kitchen, disposable plates and utensils, quick service at a counter, and a fast-moving line of customers hungry for a 20-cent shake and a 15-cent hamburger. The McDonalds had invented the future, and Kroc became their franchising agent. In 1955 he opened his own McDonald's in Des Plaines, Illinois, and franchised 200 more, then bought out the brothers in 1961. By Kroc's death in 1984, McDonald's was the largest restaurant chain in the world.

1956
New Highways

Cold War jitters about moving troops and matériel in case of a crisis helped make the case for an interstate highway system, but the real impetus was a problem that drivers faced every day: too many cars on too few roads. On June 29, President Eisenhower signed the Federal-Aid Highway Act, establishing a program in which federal gas taxes would help fund 90 percent of each highway in a 41,000-mile system. Just six weeks after the act was signed, Missouri became the first state to start construction, when workers broke ground for U.S. Route 40, now I-70 *(below)*.

Besides cutting travel time, the interstates were safer than the typical highway. They were also a boon to truckers, but the railroads, trucking's chief competitors, suffered, as did towns that were bypassed by the new routes. And, because interstates made commuting easier, they encouraged the growth of suburbs and the decline of cities.

1956
Elvis Hits
It Big

Elvis Presley had been a professional musician for two years when "Heartbreak Hotel," his first single recorded for RCA, hit the airwaves in January 1956. The song caught on with teenagers, rising to number one on the pop and country charts and number five in the rhythm and blues listings.

The 21-year-old singer had a capital year, touring 24 states, starring in his first movie, and repeatedly topping the charts. Scandalized adults called Elvis's sexy sound and onstage gyrations tasteless at best and "a new low in spiritual degeneracy" at worst. But they were hopelessly outnumbered, especially after he appeared on Ed Sullivan's highly rated prime-time variety show and converted adult viewers all over America to rock and roll. Although Fats Domino, Chuck Berry, Little Richard, and Bill Haley had earlier rock hits, it was Elvis's phenomenal success that took rock and roll from novelty to mainstream. His popularity was undimmed by his death in 1977 at age 42, and by the 1990s his fans had bought more than a billion records.

Elvis struts his stuff during an August 1956 tour of Florida (below). "He isn't afraid to express himself," a 15-year-old defender said. "When he does that on TV, I get down on the floor and scream." In Miami girls charged the stage when he sang "Hound Dog," one of several million-selling singles he released during the year (above).

1957 Showdown in Little Rock

After the Supreme Court banned school segregation *(page 122)*, many formerly all-white schools admitted black students at a snail's pace at best. Three years after the ruling, the superintendent of schools in Little Rock, Arkansas, picked nine teenagers to be the first black students at the city's Central High School, inviting them to join the 2,000 whites enrolled there. At first, Governor Orval Faubus did not object to the plan. Then, worried that segregationist political rivals might use his acquiescence against him, he reversed his position. In a move that provoked the most serious clash between a state and the federal government since the Civil War, Faubus ordered the Arkansas National Guard to keep the black students out of Central High. On September 24, President Eisenhower nationalized the guard and sent in federal troops to escort the "Little Rock Nine" into Central High School, providing a forceful demonstration that the Court's opinion must prevail, both there and throughout the country.

Under the protective eye of federal troops, the Little Rock Nine head for home. At school they faced harassment from segregationist students, as did whites who befriended them. One was expelled for turning on her tormentors; the other eight made it through.

With fixed bayonets, members of the 101st Airborne Division keep the peace at Central High. Protesters kept their distance after the soldiers clubbed an unruly white protester.

Around the World

1957
A Russian Triumph in Space

On October 4, the Soviet Union launched Sputnik, the first artificial satellite. Orbiting in a path that took it over most of Earth's populated areas (above), the 184-pound two-foot sphere had four radio antennas that broadcast a steady beep. Heard around the globe on television and radio reports, the sound was a wake-up call for most Americans, who had no idea that Soviet rocketry—and, presumably, the Soviet missile program—was so advanced. A second shock came a month later when the 1,120-pound Sputnik II went up. On board was the first space traveler, Laika, shown below in her launch couch. She orbited Earth for a week before being put to sleep by a poisoned food pellet. Scrambling to catch up, the U.S. launched a satellite of its own three months later. The space race was on.

1960
The Pill

An announcement issued by the Food and Drug Administration on May 9 signaled a revolution for American women: Physicians could now prescribe Enovid, a drug already being used to treat menstrual disorders and prevent miscarriages, as an oral contraceptive. The drug proved to be enormously popular, and for good reason, since it offered convenience and a success rate topping 98 percent, compared with 88 percent or less for other birth-control methods. By 1966 a quarter of married women under 45 were taking Enovid, as were many unmarried ones.

"The pill," as it was called, led to two key Supreme Court decisions. A 1965 ruling struck down state restrictions on the use of birth-control devices by married couples, and in 1972 the Court extended the ruling to include single people. By then, the pill had transformed American attitudes about sex, women, and the family.

1960
A TV First

On September 26, Richard M. Nixon and John F. Kennedy squared off in the first-ever televised presidential debate, an event that foreshadowed the medium's momentous role in politics. The camera loved John Kennedy. On screen he looked handsome and confident. The lens was far less kind to Nixon. He sweated heavily under hot TV lights that mercilessly revealed his nervousness and the bluish shadow of stubble on his jaw. He had a cold and, on this important night, he looked ill.

Whatever the debate's substance, millions of viewers were struck by the contrast in the candidates' looks. For them Kennedy was the clear winner. He and Nixon were to spar three more times on camera, but Kennedy never lost the impetus the first debate gave him.

Around the World

1961
The Berlin Wall Goes Up

Early in the morning of August 13, Soviet tanks clattered along the cobblestone streets of Berlin's Eastern sector, barreling toward the border with the Western zone. When the sun rose, barbed wire divided the city, marking the route where a network 28 miles long of concrete barriers and electrified fences, all heavily guarded, would soon stand.

The wall was there not to keep Westerners out, but Easterners in. Since 1949, the year that a democratic government was established in West Germany, some 2.5 million people had crossed from Communist East to capitalist West.

As the barrier rose, West Berliners gathered along it to protest its construction, only to be turned back by tear gas and water cannons. Some Easterners made frantic last dashes for the Western zone. One was the soldier shown above, whose leap over the barbed wire was caught by a photojournalist.

In Washington, hawks pushed President John F. Kennedy to confront the Soviets and stop the wall from going up. He declined. "A wall is a hell of a lot better than a war," he said.

In years to come, as many as 800 people would die trying to cross the wall, but it would stand for almost three decades, the most hated symbol of the Cold War.

1962
Americans in Space

After the humiliation of Sputnik I *(page 127)*, the United States worked hard to catch up with the Soviet space program, and in 1959 it launched Project Mercury to prepare for the first U.S. manned spaceflights. But, to the frustration of the seven top military test pilots being trained as America's first astronauts, Soviet cosmonaut Yuri Gagarin became the first man in space, making one orbit around the earth on April 12, 1961, in less than two hours. A month later, astronaut Alan Shepard Jr. became America's first man in space, completing a 15-minute suborbital flight.

Astronaut John Glenn *(right)* was the first American to attempt orbit. On February 20, 1962, an Atlas rocket boosted his *Friendship 7* capsule into outer space, where it orbited three times. The flight was a huge relief to the American public, which gave Glenn a hero's welcome comparable to that received by Charles Lindbergh 35 years before *(pages 76-77)*. America was not yet winning the space race, but it was back in the game.

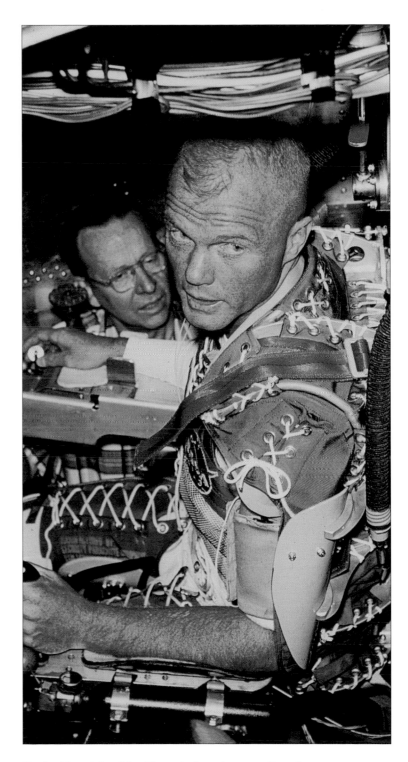

During his training, John Glenn sits in a giant centrifuge that exerts pressure on his body 16 times greater than that of ordinary gravity, simulating what he would experience when he exited and reentered Earth's atmosphere.

1962
Silent
Spring

There was a time when most Americans had never even heard the word "ecology." Then came *Silent Spring,* and the modern environmental movement was born.

The best-selling book by marine biologist Rachel Carson alerted people to the dangers of pesticides, particularly DDT. So effective was DDT at killing harmful insects that its discoverer, Paul Müller, won the Nobel Prize for medicine in 1948. It turned out, however, that it also killed fish and birds. Worse, it was further discovered that DDT built up in the fatty tissue of larger animals and was passed along in the food chain. In high concentration, it damaged the central nervous system.

The alarm sounded by *Silent Spring* spurred an awareness that resulted eventually in a ban on DDT and in a host of other reforms as people rethought the human niche in the environment.

1962
Cuban
Missile Crisis

On October 22, President Kennedy went on television during prime time to inform the nation and the world that the Soviet Union was setting up missile bases in Cuba, 90 miles off America's coast. The government had first become aware of the situation on October 14, when a U.S. spy plane spotted a missile in Cuba. Despite Soviet premier Nikita Khrushchev's claim

Fidel Castro joins Nikita Khrushchev at a rally in Moscow's Red Square in 1961, the

that he was sending only defensive weapons to his island ally, some of the bases were capable of launching intermediate-range ballistic missiles armed with nuclear warheads. America would respond, Kennedy said, by banning shipping to Cuba to make sure the military buildup stopped.

Khrushchev responded to the U.S. blockade by threatening that any American aggression against Cuba or interference with its sea lanes could ignite nuclear war, and he refused the American demand to dismantle the Cuban bases already in place. Both nations stood in full military readiness, and the world held its breath as it moved closer than ever before to the unthinkable, a nuclear confrontation.

The crisis passed on October 28 with Khrushchev's agreement to remove the weapons in exchange for America's promise not to invade Cuba and to dismantle its own missile bases in Turkey.

year of the abortive invasion of Cuba at the Bay of Pigs by U.S.-backed exiles.

1963
A Call to Feminism

What *Silent Spring* was for environmentalism, *The Feminine Mystique* was for modern feminism. The groundbreaking book by Betty Friedan held that women should have choices apart from the destiny society then decreed of being decorative, nurturing, and homebound. The book came at a time when subservience to men was considered normal and admirable and the ideal woman, as defined by the mass media, was a carefully coiffed and smiling mother. Important jobs were considered a male preserve, and three-quarters of workingwomen had female-only jobs—secretary, nurse, file clerk. Only about half as many women as men went to college.

The Feminine Mystique's argument that women should go wherever their hopes and talents take them touched a deep well of discontent. Women began to organize—in 1966, Friedan would be a founder of the National Organization for Women—and, however slowly, gender stereotypes started to crumble.

1963
The March on Washington

For citizens supporting equality and justice for African Americans, the first half of 1963 was discouraging. In April, police in Birmingham, Alabama, turned dogs and fire hoses on demonstrators seeking to desegregate lunch counters *(pages 22-23)*. Similar marches in June and July in Cambridge, Maryland, turned so violent that the governor called in the National Guard. And on June 11, NAACP leader Medgar Evers was gunned down in Jackson, Mississippi. A civil rights bill was before Congress, but powerful opponents threatened its passage *(pages 138-139)*.

Frustrated, A. Philip Randolph, president of the Brotherhood of Sleeping Car Porters, and activist Bayard Rustin called for a massive demonstration in Washington, D.C. Blacks and whites from every state responded. Carrying placards, they marched from the Washington Monument to the Lincoln Memorial. There they prayed, sang, and listened to speeches by celebrities, politicians, and civil rights leaders, the last of whom was the Reverend Martin Luther King Jr. *(left)*. The television networks carried King's address live, allowing his eloquent call for racial harmony to be heard nationwide. For millions of citizens the March on Washington was, as a white lobbyist for racial justice observed, "a beautiful expression of all that's best in America."

"I have a dream that my four little children will one day live in a nation where they will not be judged by the color of their skin but by the content of their character."

Rev. Martin Luther King Jr.

The Kennedys greet crowds at Dallas's Love Field shortly before noon. At that time the president had around an hour to live.

"I was looking . . . to the left, and I heard these terrible noises. . . . And my husband never made any sound. So I turned to the right, and all I remember is seeing my husband, he had this sort of quizzical look on his face, and his hand was up."

Jacqueline Kennedy

1963
Death of
a President

It was a political trip, a five-city swing through Texas to rally support for the 1964 presidential election. Dallas was the next-to-last stop. John Kennedy loved this sort of outing, and he had a good day for it: When Air Force One landed at the Dallas airport on the morning of November 22, the weather was crisp and glittering—no need to use the presidential limousine's bulletproof top to shield its passengers against the elements.

The welcoming crowd at Love Field was enthusiastic, especially at the sight of Jacqueline Kennedy, chic as always in a pink suit and one of her trademark pillbox hats. The friendly throngs were still larger and louder as the 24-car motorcade moved through Dallas. It rolled slowly, allowing time for the Kennedys to wave from the back of the black Lincoln where they sat behind Texas governor John Connally and his wife.

The car passed through downtown and turned right and then sharply left, slowing as it entered a park called Dealey Plaza. In the next 6.8 seconds, which were captured by a home-movie buff on film *(right)*, the world changed.

Above and behind the motorcade, from an open window on the sixth floor of a red brick building, the air cracked as a rifle bullet ripped toward the car. It hit the president in the upper back, exited through his throat, and traveled on, wounding Connally. Another bullet found the right rear quadrant of Kennedy's head, which exploded in a spray of blood, brain, and bone.

The president slumped against his wife as his limousine roared toward nearby Parkland Hospital. There, at 12:55 p.m., John Fitzgerald Kennedy died. As shock and grief spread from Dallas throughout the nation, police within hours arrested a misfit named Lee Harvey Oswald for the murder. Before his full story could be

Already injured, President Kennedy jerks his hands to his throat in the photo at top, part of a film made by spectator Abraham Zapruder. Mrs. Kennedy cradles her husband in the second frame, moments before a second bullet hits him (third from top). At bottom, a Secret Service agent reaches out to Mrs. Kennedy.

Aboard Air Force One shortly after the assassination, Lyndon Johnson takes the oath of office as the nation's 36th president from federal judge Sarah Hughes. He is flanked by his wife, Lady Bird, and Jacqueline Kennedy.

Jack Ruby shoots and kills suspected assassin Lee Harvey Oswald in the basement garage of the Dallas police station. Convicted of murder and then granted a retrial on appeal, Ruby died while awaiting his second trial.

told, Oswald himself was gunned down by a strip-joint owner, Jack Ruby, who claimed that he acted to spare Mrs. Kennedy the trauma of testifying at Oswald's trial. The years to come would bring endless speculation on whether Oswald, and perhaps Ruby, had been part of an assassination conspiracy.

That drama had not yet begun to play out, though, as millions watched on television the grave splendor of the president's funeral in Washington. It left indelible images. For many Americans, the most poignant was the sleek black horse that marched riderless behind the president's caisson-borne casket, empty boots turned backward in the stirrups, the age-old symbol of a fallen leader.

John F. Kennedy Jr. salutes his father's coffin outside Saint Matthew's Cathedral.

The funeral cortege crosses the Potomac River to Arlington National Cemetery on the by three pairs of matched gray horses. It took one hour for the three-mile-long proces-

> "It was clear and cold that day. . . . The sky was sparkling blue. . . . And then there was the coffin with a flag that seemed to have redder reds and whiter whites than I had ever seen."
>
> Roger Wilkins

hilly Virginia shore. The president's flag-draped casket was carried on a caisson drawn sion to travel from Saint Matthew's Cathedral in Washington to the cemetery.

After the burial, Jacqueline Kennedy holds the flag that covered her husband's coffin.

1964
The Beatles Invade

Rock and roll was stagnant and spirits were low in post-assassination America when a fresh breeze blew in from across the Atlantic. Their names were John, Paul, George, and Ringo —the Beatles, collectively—and they had blitzed Britain before traveling to the United States for their first tour. Beatlemania broke out all over America when the group performed on the *Ed Sullivan Show* on February 9, and *Meet the Beatles,* the group's first album released here, shot to number one on the charts.

At first, the Mop Tops' success was more a matter of hair than harmonies—in style and attitude, they were the very embodiment of the new culture bursting on the youth scene. But they reenergized American rock and opened the way for other British invaders, including the Rolling Stones and the Who. Eventually honored as artists, the Beatles' songs proved more influential and lasting than those of any of their musical peers.

1964
The End of Jim Crow

Racism infected all of America in the 1960s, but only in the South was it enshrined in law. Thus it was perhaps ironic, or perhaps inevitable, that a southerner, hardscrabble Texan Lyndon Baines Johnson, would end the collection of injustices known as Jim Crow, the laws condemning southern blacks to second-class citizenship and continual humiliation.

John Kennedy had proposed a civil rights law before his death. But for all his vibrant style, he lacked his rough-hewn successor's talent for congressional maneuvering. When it came to cajoling, prom-

Separate and unequal facilities were a way of life under Jim Crow laws. If it could not

ising, threatening, and bullying a bill through Congress, President Johnson had no equal. He knew well the indignities that African Americans endured under Jim Crow laws, and he made civil rights a priority.

After a long struggle that climaxed with choking off a record three-month filibuster led by southern Democrats in the Senate, Johnson signed the 1964 Civil Rights Act on July 2. The sweeping measure outlawed racial discrimination in restaurants, theaters, hotels, and other public accommodations. It also empowered the Justice Department to end legal segregation in public places such as schools and hospitals.

Thanks to an opponent's strategic blunder, the law banned discrimination in employment on the basis of sex as well as race. Representative Howard Smith of Virginia inserted the gender issue into the bill, hoping to garner enough antifeminist votes to kill it entirely. But the bill passed, and Smith's miscalculation ensured that both blacks and women would thenceforth be protected by federal law.

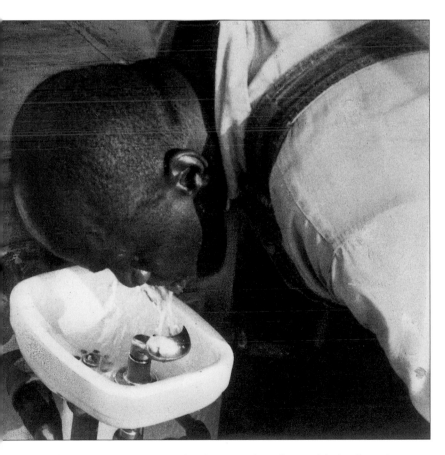

in itself end racism, the 1964 Civil Rights Act at least destroyed its legal sanction.

1964 New Left Protest

The discontent with the status quo that was beginning to seethe on college campuses drew young veterans of the civil rights struggle to a meeting in Port Huron, Michigan, in 1962. There they organized Students for a Democratic Society, whose manifesto decrying militarism, racial injustice, and poverty defined the philosophy of what was called the New Left.

New Leftists first gained broad national attention and new followers in 1964, when administrators at the University of California at Berkeley banned on-campus recruiting of civil rights workers and fund-raising for the movement. The ban ignited the Free Speech Movement (FSM), which staged protracted protests culminating with a huge sit-in and the arrest of some 800 people. Widespread sympathy for the demonstrators assured them of the broader political rights they sought. The FSM became the model for campus protest, but the issue of free speech soon paled before a more pressing matter of student concern: the Vietnam War.

Marines of the Ninth Expeditionary Brigade come ashore on Red Beach Two at Da Nang, South Vietnam, on March 8.

"In the name of freedom, America is mutilating Vietnam. In the name of peace, America turns that . . . country into a wasteland. And in the name of democracy, America is burying its own dreams. . . . "

Leaflet, Students for a Democratic Society

1965
Escalation
in Vietnam

The most divisive war in modern U.S. history escalated without ever even being declared. In August of 1964, Congress ceded its authority to declare war by passing the Gulf of Tonkin Resolution. Approved in response to alleged aggression in the gulf by North Vietnamese torpedo boats, the resolution empowered President Lyndon Johnson to broaden the conflict virtually at will.

At the time, there were some 16,000 American military advisers in South Vietnam. But by the following May, Johnson, who had been promising that Americans would not die fighting an Asian war, had sent 30,000 more troops to Vietnam. Within three years the number would pass half a million. And as the war intensified, so did the draft, spiraling up in the mid-1960s from about 100,000 to 300,000 men annually.

The escalation focused and radicalized domestic dissent. College campuses erupted in demonstrations, many led by veterans of the civil rights and free-speech movements *(pages 132-133, 139)*. Before long the protests, ever larger and more confrontational, were spilling into the streets. There were public draft-card burnings as thousands of young men defied or avoided conscription. Some antiwar demonstrations drew as many as half a million people—New Leftists, traditional liberals and pacifists, and an assortment of those who thought the war immoral, unwinnable, or just tragically wasteful.

Hardly any American was untouched by the war: not the demonstrators, their sympathizers, their detractors, not the young men fighting and dying in Asia, thousands of miles from home.

A medical evacuation helicopter flies in to pick up wounded soldiers of the 173rd Airborne Brigade. The troops had been ambushed during a search-and-destroy mission in the Iron Triangle area near Saigon in October.

1965
"We Shall Overcome"

Though the right to vote is guaranteed by the Constitution, a long history of discriminatory practices such as literacy tests prevented the vast majority of blacks in the South from even registering. To dramatize the issue, early in 1965 civil rights protesters tried to march from Selma, Alabama, to the state capitol in Montgomery. They were thwarted by authorities wielding clubs and tear gas until protection by federalized National Guardsmen allowed completion of the 54-mile march.

President Lyndon B. Johnson seized upon Selma to promote the Voting Rights Act. Echoing the civil rights anthem, he told the nation on television, "We shall overcome." Passed in August, the act dramatically increased black registration. In Selma, it brought the defeat in 1968 of Jim Clark, the country sheriff who only three years before had been beating people who wanted to vote.

Civil rights marchers stride along between Selma and Montgomery. In the capital their

ranks swelled to 25,000, making the demonstration the largest in the South's history.

1966
A Warning
to Smokers

One-half of U.S. men and nearly one-third of women smoked cigarettes in the 1960s, and they did it practically everywhere, without embarrassment. Smoking had been made chic by advertising showing rugged cowboys and medical doctors who said a cigarette was good for soothing jangled nerves. But in 1964 a 150,000-word report by a panel of 10 researchers appointed by the U.S. surgeon general confirmed what many physicians and scientists had long insisted: The habit was a major cause of lung cancer, emphysema, and heart disease.

Congress required manufacturers to place a warning label on each pack of cigarettes beginning in 1966: "Caution: Cigarette Smoking May Be Hazardous to Your Health." By the late 1990s the habit was so frowned upon that those who still practiced it—nearly 25 percent of adults—frequently had to sneak their smokes.

1966
Rights for the Accused

The words became familiar to every policeman making an arrest and every viewer of TV cop shows: "You have a right to remain silent. Any statement you make may be used in evidence against you. . . ." This legal ritual began with Ernesto Miranda, a 23-year-old Arizona high-school dropout who was picked out of a police lineup and interrogated about a rape and kidnapping. Miranda confessed to the crime and was convicted, but his lawyers appealed all the way to the Supreme Court, arguing that the police had failed to inform Miranda that the Fifth Amendment protected him against self-incrimination. On June 6 the Court overturned Miranda's conviction. One lawman complained, "I guess now we'll have to supply all squad cars with attorneys." But civil libertarians declared that the decision affirmed the constitutional rights not only of the accused but of all Americans.

THE FOLLOWING WARNING MUST BE READ TO A SUBJECT BEFORE INTERROGATION

114.24.16

1. You have a right to remain silent, the Constitution requires that I so inform you of this right and you need not talk to me if you do not wish to do so. You do not have to answer any of my questions.

2. Should you talk to me, anything which you might say in answer to my questions can and will be introduced into evidence in court against you.

3. If you want an attorney to be present at this time or anytime hereafter, you are entitled to such counsel. If you cannot afford to pay for counsel, we will furnish you with counsel if you so desire.

4. Knowing your rights as I have just related them to you, are you now willing to answer my questions without having an attorney present?

1967
The First Super Bowl

In the beginning, despite the souped-up name, it was merely a championship football game. The first Super Bowl matched the champions of the two professional leagues that recently had agreed to merge: the Green Bay Packers of the old National Football League and the Kansas City Chiefs of the upstart American Football League. To no one's great surprise, the veteran league prevailed. Green Bay won 35-10 on the coaching genius of Vince Lombardi and the stalwart passing of quarterback Bart Starr (right).

Lombardi was renowned for the remark "Winning isn't everything—it's the only thing." But it was an entrepreneur, Sonny

"Winning isn't everything—it's the only thing."

Vince Lombardi

Werblin, owner of the New York Jets, who saw that "football is show business." That first Super Bowl was a milestone in the meteoric rise of professional sports as entertainment. Major league franchises in football and basketball more than doubled during the decade; baseball's franchises increased by 25 percent. Thanks to television, revenues rocketed, and so did the salaries of a new breed of superstars. The Super Bowl set the pace. It became an every-January institution, an unofficial national holiday, each one designated by the appropriate Roman numeral.

Green Bay quarterback Bart Starr uncorks a pass as Kansas City lineman Buck Buchanan moves in on him. Starr was named the game's most valuable player.

1967
Hero of the
Little Man

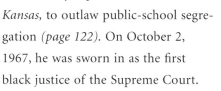

His great-grandfather was a slave, his father a railroad porter, his mother a teacher in a segregated school. At Howard University Law School, where he graduated first in his class, Thurgood Marshall "found out what my rights were." In 1954, as director of the NAACP Legal Defense and Educational Fund, he persuaded the Supreme Court in *Brown v. the Board of Education of Topeka, Kansas,* to outlaw public-school segregation *(page 122)*. On October 2, 1967, he was sworn in as the first black justice of the Supreme Court.

In his 24 years on the Court, he championed the little man. Marshall "imparted not only his legal acumen, but also his life experiences," wrote his colleague Sandra Day O'Connor, whom President Reagan appointed the first woman justice in 1981, "constantly pushing and prodding us to respond not only to the persuasiveness of legal argument, but also to the power of moral truth."

1968
The Tet Offensive

Nearly three years after the entry of U.S. troops into South Vietnam, the word on the war from Washington was "steady progress." Close to half a million Americans fought in the South, and more bombs had been dropped on North Vietnam than on the enemy during all of World War II. In Saigon, the U.S. commander, General William Westmoreland, saw "light at the end of the tunnel."

Both sides had agreed to a cease-fire for Tet, the holiday that began the lunar new year on January 30, 1968. But the night before, Radio Hanoi broadcast a prearranged signal to Communist forces—a poem by leader Ho Chi Minh honoring the arrival of the Year of the Monkey. Within hours of the broadcast, the first of some 70,000 Communist troops struck. They attacked more than 100 targets throughout the South, and fighting raged for three weeks before U.S. and South Vietnamese troops finally restored order. The Tet offensive failed militarily. It cost the lives of perhaps half of the attacking force and failed to capture any city or stir a general uprising.

But Tet was a strategic success. Brought home in images like the photograph shown at left, the energy of an enemy alleged to be on the run stunned even Americans who had supported the war and thought the United States had the upper hand. In the New Hampshire Democratic presidential primary in early March, antiwar Senator Eugene McCarthy of Minnesota made a very strong showing against President Lyndon Johnson, who was a write-in candidate. On March 31, Johnson, shown at right pondering a draft of his speech, went on television to announce a partial halt in the bombing of North Vietnam—and his decision not to seek reelection.

U.S. Marines wounded during the Tet attacks are evacuated from Hue on a tank. It took more than three weeks of bombing and shelling to dislodge the enemy, who briefly established a revolutionary government in the city.

"... I do not believe that I should devote an hour or a day of my time to any personal partisan causes. ... Accordingly, I shall not seek, and will not accept, the nomination of my party for another term. ..."

Lyndon B. Johnson, March 31

1968
The Assassination of Dr. King

The man who, more than any other, had awakened the hope of blacks and pricked the conscience of whites in America died on April 4, the victim of a bigot's bullet. The Reverend Dr. Martin Luther King Jr., the inspirational leader of the nation's civil rights struggle since the Montgomery bus boycott more than a decade before *(page 123)*, was in Memphis to support a strike by the city's predominantly black sanitation workers. He was talking with colleagues on the balcony of his motel when he was shot. Police quickly arrested James Earl Ray, a white supremacist who in 1969 would be convicted of the assassination and sentenced to 99 years in prison.

An apostle of nonviolence, King had espoused passive resistance to root out racial injustice. Ironically, his death ignited riots in more than 100 U.S. cities and exacerbated one of the most tumultuous eras in American history. In the wake of the killing, leadership of the civil rights movement would pass to more militant men, but King would remain its most powerful symbol, the emblem of its most heroic days.

On the balcony of the Lorraine Motel, followers of Martin Luther King Jr. stand over their dying leader, pointing toward the fatal bullet's source. One of the men kneels beside King, trying to stanch blood flowing from his neck.

1968
The Killing of Robert Kennedy

Two months after the assassination of Martin Luther King Jr., another champion of the dispossessed was killed. On June 6, Senator Robert F. Kennedy (*below*) was gunned down in a hallway of a Los Angeles hotel by Sirhan Sirhan, an Arab nationalist angered by Kennedy's support for Israel.

A late but potent entry into the 1968 presidential race, Kennedy had declared victory in the crucial California primary just before his assassination. He was running on a platform of achieving racial equity, attacking poverty, and ending the Vietnam War. His death dashed the dreams of those who saw in him his slain brother's worthiest successor and the best hope of uniting a nation in crisis.

1968
Democratic National Convention

In late August, American political and social discontent erupted for all the world to see as Democrats gathered to nominate a presidential candidate at their national convention in Chicago. As delegates convened inside the International Amphitheater, some 10,000 demonstrators—most of them young, most of them concerned mainly with ending the Vietnam War—assembled outside, where they faced a force of 12,000 Chicago police in riot gear. The ensuing week-long conflict, later described as a "police riot" by a national commission, would see hundreds of protesters, journalists, and bystanders beaten and tear-gassed. Television cameras recorded much of the mayhem as dissidents chanted, "The whole world is watching." The bloodletting in Chicago would cripple the Democrats in the coming campaign and help assure the election of Richard M. Nixon as president.

1969
Man on the Moon

I believe that this nation should commit itself," President Kennedy told Congress on May 25, 1961, "to achieving the goal, before this decade is out, of landing a man on the Moon and returning him safely to earth." The National Aeronautics and Space Administration (NASA) heeded his call, investing $24 billion and the labor of more than 450,000 workers in Project Apollo. In December 1968, with just a year left to reach the goal the president had set, Apollo astronauts orbited the Moon for the first time.

On July 16, 1969, some one million spectators crowded the roads and beaches around Cape Kennedy, Florida, hoping to witness the beginning of the greatest adventure of all time. Apollo 11 astronauts Neil Armstrong, Edwin "Buzz" Aldrin Jr., and Michael Collins, wearing the Apollo emblem below, blasted off into space. Four days later, while Collins remained in orbit aboard the command module *Columbia,* Armstrong and Aldrin dropped downward toward the Moon in the landing vehicle *Eagle.* Realizing that their automatic navigation system was steering them toward a huge crater, Armstrong grabbed the controls and brought the craft down safely on the smooth Sea of Tranquillity. He emerged from the hatch and switched on a television camera attached to *Eagle* to record his historic first steps on the powdery surface. A quarter million miles away, some 600 million TV viewers watched in awe as he announced, "That's one small step for man, one giant leap for mankind."

With five months to spare, NASA had fulfilled Kennedy's vision. On the grave of the slain president in Arlington National Cemetery a bunch of flowers appeared, along with a note, "Mr. President, the *Eagle* has landed."

Buzz Aldrin descends Eagle's ladder. He and Armstrong spent about two and a half hours on the Moon, conducting scientific experiments and collecting soil samples.

1969
Woodstock Festival

Woodstock—which was not even at Woodstock—was the beatific summation of the peace-and-love generation. Promoters had planned the three-day mid-August music festival for the New York Catskills town, then moved it to Max Yasgur's 600-acre farm outside the nearby village of White Lake. No matter. Woodstock it would remain to the 400,000 counterculture enthusiasts who were there, and who would remember it forever.

Expecting only a fraction of that throng, the organizers found their modest facilities for food, water, and sanitation overwhelmed, and rainstorms turned the farm's grassy fields to mud. But despite overcrowding, hardships, and too many drugs, amity reigned. Not a single fight marred the bliss as celebrants rocked with Janis Joplin, Jimi Hendrix, and other superstars. The event was destined to pass into American legend, its beatific glow undimmed.

1970
Death at Kent State

Richard Nixon had campaigned for president on a promise to end the long and corrosive war in Vietnam. On April 30 he escalated it, sending U.S. troops pouring into Cambodia. The move would prove futile militarily and combustible at home, where millions opposed the war.

Campuses erupted in outrage. At Kent State University in Ohio, militant protests peaked on Saturday night, May 2, when someone set fire to the college ROTC building. In response, Ohio's governor ordered in the National Guard.

Monday found about 500 unarmed students facing about 75 guardsmen bearing tear gas and rifles. Several protesters threw rocks. The troops answered with tear gas, and then some of them opened fire, killing four students and wounding nine more. Two of the four dead were protesters; the other two were young women on their way to class.

The Kent State debacle widened the national rift over the war, further eroding public support and radicalizing dissent.

Mourner Mary Ann Vecchio wails over the body of Kent State student Jeffrey Miller in

a photograph that would become a banner of vengeance for the antiwar movement.

1971 Pentagon Papers

In 1967, Defense Secretary Robert McNamara commissioned a top-secret study of American involvement in Vietnam and the rest of Indochina since World War II. It painted U.S. leadership as inept at best, cynical and dishonest at worst.

The 7,000-page study remained under wraps until 1971, when Daniel Ellsberg, a former Pentagon analyst, leaked it to the *New York Times*. When the *Times* began running articles based on it in June, the Nixon administration got a court order to stop publication, claiming a threat to national security. However, Ellsberg provided the *Washington Post* with the Pentagon Papers, as they came to be called, and the revelations continued.

In a landmark decision favoring the press, the Supreme Court ruled against the government because it could not prove in advance that publishing the Pentagon Papers would cause harm to the nation. Along with curbing the government's ability to suppress the news, the affair was another coal on the blaze of antiwar sentiment in America.

1972
Nixon in China

It was a stunning policy reversal: In February, a president of the United States traveled to the Communist People's Republic of China, where he dined with its leaders (*above*) and offered his nation's friendship. As an arch anti-Communist, Richard Nixon seemed an unlikely fence-mender. However, his concerns about China's potential for enormous industrial power overcame his political scruples. Unless hostilities were softened, he said, the Asian giant might become the "most formidable enemy that has ever existed in the history of the world."

The fruit of Nixon's journey was a communiqué in which China and the United States resolved to improve relations. It was the greatest foreign policy coup of his presidency.

1973
Legalizing Abortion

Her name was Norma McCorvey. She was a Dallas waitress, young, poor, single—and pregnant. She wanted an abortion, but in Texas, as in most of America, abortion was illegal unless the mother's life was endangered by the pregnancy. The dilemma was not especially unusual, but the outcome was, for Norma McCorvey, under the alias of Jane Roe, would occasion one of the most far-reaching and controversial decisions in the history of the U.S. Supreme Court: the judgment allowing most women to terminate an unwanted pregnancy.

The Court's seven-to-two ruling, based on the right to privacy in the First Amendment, declared that no state can interfere with a woman's decision to abort during the first six months of pregnancy. Going to the heart of the matter, the judgment in the case of *Roe v. Wade* also declared that a fetus is not regarded as a person under the Constitution and thus has no legal entitlement to life.

The ruling prompted passionate reaction, since it dealt with one of the most emotional and divisive social issues of American life, one in which opinions were clearly drawn and deeply held. Prolife forces, horrified by the decision, argued that life begins at conception, that abortion is therefore murder, that the state has a duty to protect the unborn, and that abortion encourages promiscuity. On the other side, prochoice advocates held that a woman's right to control her own body is basic and must not be subject to governmental interference. They also argued that criminalizing abortion often left women, especially poor women, with no option but to risk being maimed or killed by back-alley abortionists.

While *Roe v. Wade* decided the legality of abortion, the debate over its morality continued to rage. In an odd footnote to the conflict, Norma McCorvey—Jane Roe—rethought her position years after the Court's ruling, in 1995 taking a stand against abortions after the first trimester of pregnancy.

1973
Leaving Vietnam

For America, it was over. On January 27, representatives of the United States and North Vietnam signed a cease-fire agreement in Paris. The last U.S. ground troops started home. And President Richard Nixon declared, "We have finally achieved peace with honor." But at home there was no rejoicing in the streets. America responded with weary apathy to the end of a 10-year conflict that had cost so much: the nation's innocence, its belief in its invincibility, the lives of 57,000 of its young men.

Two years after the U.S.-North Vietnamese cease-fire, the last shots were fired in the war to stop Communism in Vietnam, as the country united under a Communist regime.

"It isn't peace. And there is no honor."

A returning Vietnam veteran

Lieutenant Colonel Robert L. Stirm, a returning prisoner of war, is reunited with his family. Peace did mean joy for the loved ones of 653 American POWs released by Hanoi under the cease-fire agreement. Of the 24,000 U.S. servicemen stationed in Vietnam when the agreement was signed, all but a tiny fraction, including 159 marine embassy guards, were evacuated within two months.

Charles W. Colson

E. Howard Hunt Jr.

G. Gordon Liddy

H. R. Haldeman

Jeb Stuart Magruder

John W. Dean III

John D. Ehrlichman

John N. Mitchell

Fourteen top Nixon administration officials, including the eight shown above, were jailed or fined after being convicted or pleading guilty on Watergate-related charges.

1973
The Watergate
Hearings

White House Press Secretary Ronald L. Ziegler dismissed it as a "third-rate burglary attempt." But the 1972 break-in at the Democratic National Committee headquarters in Washington's Watergate building by men working for Richard Nixon's reelection campaign was also the metaphor for a panoply of evils that befouled his presidency. By May 1973 the Watergate scandal had grown big enough to prompt Senate com-

> "I don't give a s--- what happens. I want you all to stonewall it, let them plead the Fifth Amendment, cover up or anything else if it'll save . . . the plan."

Richard Nixon to aides, taped conversation, March 22, 1973

mittee hearings. Stretching into the summer, the televised hearings would reveal a White House awash in criminality and chicanery that included abuse of power, illegal wiretapping, burglary, dirty tricks, enemies' lists, secret slush funds, money laundering, character assassination, and obstruction of justice.

The most damning witness was John W. Dean III, former counsel to the president, shown at right being sworn before the committee. The Nixon camp tried to discredit Dean, but another witness, Alexander Butterfield, revealed that the president had secretly taped all his Oval Office conversations. The contents of those tapes would corroborate Dean's sordid story.

1973
The Energy Crisis

Americans, used to cheap gasoline and lots of it, were appalled to find themselves waiting in long lines to pay soaring prices for gasoline—if it was available at all. At the same time, householders put on sweaters and lowered their thermostats to conserve heating oil.

The roots of the crisis lay in the oil-rich Middle East, where in October war erupted between Israelis and Arabs. The Arab-dominated Organization of Petroleum Exporting Countries (OPEC) drastically hiked prices while cutting production and embargoed exports to countries supporting Israel, including the United States.

The embargo was lifted after six months, but the energy crisis left an indelible mark. Higher oil prices abruptly dampened the economic boom the nation had enjoyed in the post-World War II years, and American optimism about an ever rising tide of prosperity began to dim.

1974
Nixon Resigns

Throughout the Watergate scandal, Richard Nixon strove mightily to deny investigators access to the Oval Office audiotapes that he himself had made of his official conversations *(pages 156-157)*. When the tapes began coming to light, his cause for concern was clear. They showed that whatever his gifts, Nixon had a dark side—that he was cynical, deceitful, vicious, vengeful, paranoid, petty, profane, bigoted. They also showed that he had abused federal powers and obstructed justice: Only six days

---

"I have never been a quitter. To leave office before my term is completed is opposed to every instinct in my body."

Richard Nixon, resignation speech, August 8

---

after the abortive Watergate burglary, he had ordered the CIA to thwart an FBI probe of the case.

Faced with certain impeachment by the House of Representatives and likely conviction by the Senate, on August 8 Nixon announced to the nation in a televised speech that he would resign, becoming the first president in American history to do so. A preemptive pardon by his successor, Gerald R. Ford, spared him the further indignity of a possible criminal indictment.

As a sort of elder statesman, Nixon would gain a measure of redemption in later years. Even so, the ugliness of Watergate had shaken America's faith in its leaders, perhaps permanently.

Shortly before his August 9 resignation becomes official, Richard Nixon says farewell to his White House staff as his tearful wife, Pat, looks on.

> "We are reaching the stage where the problems that we must solve are going to become insoluble without computers. I do not fear computers. I fear the lack of them."
>
> Isaac Asimov

The Apple II above is hooked to a TV set and, at left, two disk drives, which in 1978 replaced the cassette recorder used initially to store data. A pair of game-controller paddles were part of the Apple II package.

1977
The PC Boots Up

With the introduction of the Apple II in April, computers began beeping out of the esoteric and into the everyday. The Altair 8800 of 1975—the first device that could be called a personal computer—had been an assembly-required affair, intended for afficionados. The Apple II, on the other hand, was for a mass market of nonexperts. It was about the size of a typewriter, weighed only 12 pounds, sported an integrated keyboard and a four-kilobyte memory, and was fully assembled. To store data it had to be hooked up to a cassette recorder, and it used a television set as a monitor, either color or black and white. The price was a steep $1,298.

Dazzling at the time, the Apple II would soon seem primitive as hundreds of companies rushed to compete with Apple for a share of the new market and made constant refinements. Technology flourished and prices fell, making home computers increasingly accessible. Within 10 years of the Apple II's advent, computers were in 25 million homes, schools, and offices. They were projected to be in 70 percent of America's households by century's end. Most would be linked to the Internet, which offered a vast cache of data and diversion, and to each other, permitting electronic mail *(page 178)*.

The computer was changing the way people communicated and played, and also how they worked and learned. It facilitated working at home, and telecommuting became increasingly popular: Fourteen million Americans were expected to be home based by the year 2000. And the trend seemed likely to continue, for while the computer remained a persistent mystery to some adults, it was commonplace to the generation growing up with it. As the new millennium neared, 91 percent of America's teachers of kindergarten through the sixth grade were using it in the classroom.

1977
Star Wars and Star Wares

The word among Hollywood insiders was that director George Lucas's *Star Wars* was going to flop. But then it opened and became, almost instantly, much more than a blockbuster. It was a cultural icon, a phenomenon of faith: In a cynical age, Lucas had given America a myth.

Critics praised the space fantasy's breathtaking special effects and breakneck action, but most of all they liked its purity, its simple innocence of vision. The young loved it, and so did the old. In the adventures of Luke Skywalker, Princess Leia, Han Solo, and their various quirky sidekicks, Lucas gave assurance that loyalty and courage conquer all odds, that good triumphs over evil.

Good also sells, as movie executives and marketers quickly discovered. *Star Wars* earned more than any film in history, and it revolutionized movie merchandising: Before it, merchandise had been promotional gimmickry in service of the film; now it was an end in itself. In two decades, products based on *Star Wars* and its two sequels—posters, sheets, cups, kits, clothes, books, video games—earned $2.6 billion. And the appeal of the heroes and villains was as fresh as ever: In 1997 *Star Wars* action figures were the best-selling toys for American boys.

Lovable robots C-3PO and R2D2 (left) almost upstaged Star Wars' human heroes.

Around the World

1978
The Camp David
Peace Accords

In September, after nearly two weeks of cloistered talks brokered by Jimmy Carter (above, center) at Camp David, his presidential retreat, Egyptian president Anwar el-Sadat (above, right) and Israeli premier Menachem Begin (above, left) agreed on a framework to end 30 years of hostility between Israel and its Arab neighbors.

Carter's personal diplomacy proved crucial to the summit's success. When Begin and Sadat reached an impasse, he met with them individually and worked out a compromise. Begin later remarked, "It was really the Jimmy Carter conference."

Sadat and Begin shared the 1978 Nobel Peace Prize for their efforts, and in 1979 they signed a formal treaty between their nations. But peace remained elusive. Many Arabs were angered by Sadat's concessions, and in 1981 he was assassinated by radical Muslim fundamentalists. As the century drew to a close, conflict still roiled the Middle East. Nevertheless, the Camp David accords kept hopes for an eventual resolution alive.

1979
Three Mile Island

On March 28, a crisis erupted at the Three Mile Island nuclear power plant near Harrisburg, Pennsylvania *(below)*. A faulty valve in the cooling system of one of the plant's reactors caused coolant to stop circulating in the nuclear core, in which uranium fission produces energy. The core shut down as it was designed to do, but technicians misdiagnosed the problem and compounded it by draining the coolant. The core overheated, and a meltdown seemed imminent. In addition, a bubble of hydrogen gas inside the reactor raised the specter of a massive explosion. Pregnant women and children were evacuated from the area to prevent their exposure to leaking radioactive gases, and thousands of other residents fled.

By April 2 the malfunctioning reactor was under control, and and on April 9 the Nuclear Regulatory Commission declared that the crisis at Three Mile Island was over. Nevertheless, the doubts it raised about the safety of nuclear power hurt the industry, and in the next two decades no permit for the construction of a nuclear power plant was approved.

1981
The Reagan Revolution

I t's the first time I ever voted Republican," said one Michigan voter. "But I'm sick and tired of the mess that's going on in this country." Supported by many who felt the same way, former actor and governor Ronald Reagan handily defeated President Jimmy Carter in November 1980. Staunchly conservative, Reagan blamed liberal "big government" for the malaise and inflation of the 1970s. "Liberalism is no longer the answer," he proclaimed. "It is the problem."

Inaugurated in January 1981, he soon began what reporters called "the Reagan revolution"—a combination of higher military spending, lower taxes, and cutbacks in domestic programs. It paid off in a six-year economic expansion, the longest one America had yet enjoyed in peacetime. According to many historians, the military buildup also helped end the Cold War, convincing the ailing Soviet Union that it could not afford to keep up. During the same period, however, poor Americans lost ground badly, with homelessness becoming a major issue for the first time since the Depression. And because taxes could not cover all the military spending, America's national debt and annual budget deficit became the largest in history.

Whatever history's verdict may be on such outcomes, Reagan's political achievement was clear. With a combination of Hollywood charm and bedrock conservative beliefs, he brought to a close five decades of government activism that had begun in 1933 with Franklin Roosevelt's New Deal *(pages 86-87)* and had marked every administration, Republican and Democratic alike. A new era had arrived.

> "Government is not the solution to our problem; government is the problem."
>
> Ronald Reagan, inaugural address, January 20

Looking characteristically genial and upbeat, Reagan addresses an audience in 1982. Even staunch Democrats who opposed his policies were beguiled by his appealing manner.

1981
The Hostage Crisis

Just hours after being sworn in on January 20 *(page 163)*, President Ronald Reagan had a happy announcement to make: Fifty-two Americans who had been held hostage in Iran for the past 444 days were coming home. So ended a crisis that made the United States look powerless before the world and helped unseat President Carter.

The scene for crisis was set in 1978, when revolutionaries deposed the Shah of Iran, a longtime U.S. ally. When the United States admitted the hated shah to receive cancer treatment in 1979, anti-American feeling boiled over, and militants overran the U.S. embassy and seized the hostages.

Despite stringent sanctions imposed by President Carter, Iran was unyielding until the shah's death in 1980 opened the way for negotiations and the hostages' homecoming. After it ended, the crisis still cast a long shadow, inspiring Middle Eastern terrorist groups to use hostages as leverage for their cause.

Militants crowd around a hostage on public display outside the American embassy.

1981
The AIDS Epidemic

The first news accounts were easy to miss. On June 5, 1981, the Centers for Disease Control announced that a rare type of pneumonia had been diagnosed in five homosexual men. A month later, the *New York Times* reported on a rare cancer afflicting 41 men, most of them gay. The stories pointed the way to a global medical disaster. By 1982 it had a name: AIDS, acquired immune deficiency syndrome, and a year later scientists discovered its

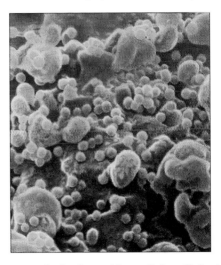

cause—the human immunodeficiency virus (HIV), shown here in an electron microphotograph as green particles inside an immune cell *(yellow)*. The disease weakened the immune system, causing an infected person to develop one ailment after another. As far as doctors could tell, a diagnosis was a death sentence; the body could not fight off the infection.

There were an estimated 1,600 cases worldwide in 1982; six years later, there were 250,000. People with AIDS included homosexual men, drug users, blood-transfusion recipients, African and Haitian heterosexuals—and, potentially, everyone else. The fact that AIDS was often transmitted through gay sex at first limited public sympathy and medical research efforts, but the widespread indifference and outright hostility toward AIDS sufferers began to fade as the epidemic spread.

By the late 1990s, 31 million people in the world carried the human immunodeficiency virus. Expensive medicines could help victims live much longer, but there was still no vaccine or cure.

1982
A Healing Wall

Before its completion, the Vietnam Veterans Memorial stirred controversy. The design—a V-shaped wall of black marble engraved with the names of the more than 58,000 Americans who were killed in Vietnam or died later from their wounds—seemed insultingly stark to some veterans still smarting from wartime protests and a lack of homefront support. But after "the Wall," as it came to be known, was dedicated on November 13, that feeling changed. Tourists, quiet and respectful, soon made it among the most visited sites in Washington, D.C. The high volume of visitors continued in the years that followed, as two sculptures—one of three servicemen, the other a tribute to women who served—were added nearby. Honoring the dead without judging the war itself, the memorial came to symbolize a new era of national reconciliation. Since the Wall's dedication, visitors have left more than 50,000 personal mementos, two of which are shown at right.

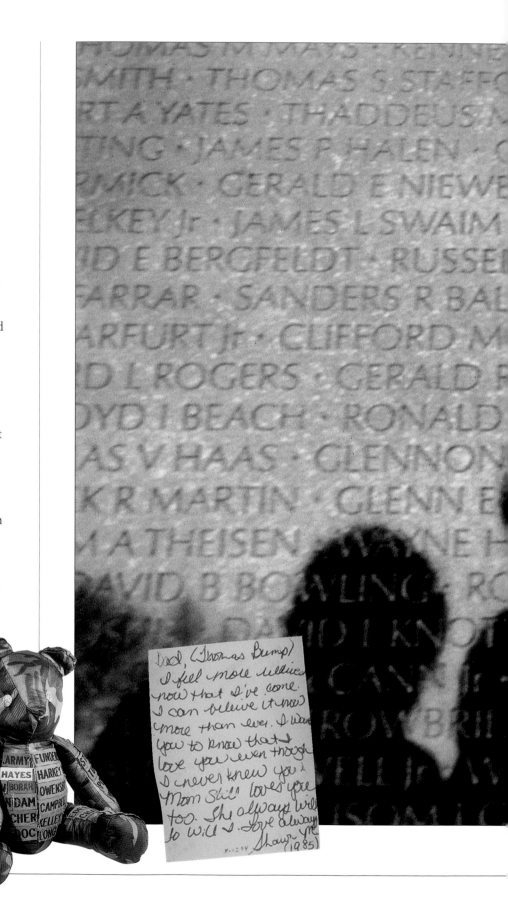

1984
Top Hit:
Thriller

At five, he became lead singer of the Jackson 5, a group of brothers from Gary, Indiana. He was 11 when in 1969 they cut their first Motown single, a teenager as they sold millions of records. But Michael Jackson was never meant to be just one of the crowd. In 1979 his solo album *Off the Wall,* which fielded four top-10 hits including "Rock With You" and "Don't Stop 'Til You Get Enough," was one of the year's bestsellers. It was a monster accomplishment, but it paled in comparison with his 1982 follow-up, *Thriller.* It won an unprecedented eight Grammy awards, and the video showcasing Jackson's catlike, sensuous dancing helped propel the year-old MTV music channel to new heights of popularity. In 1984 *Thriller* became the best-selling album in history, with more than 30 million copies sold.

1986
The Explosion
of Challenger

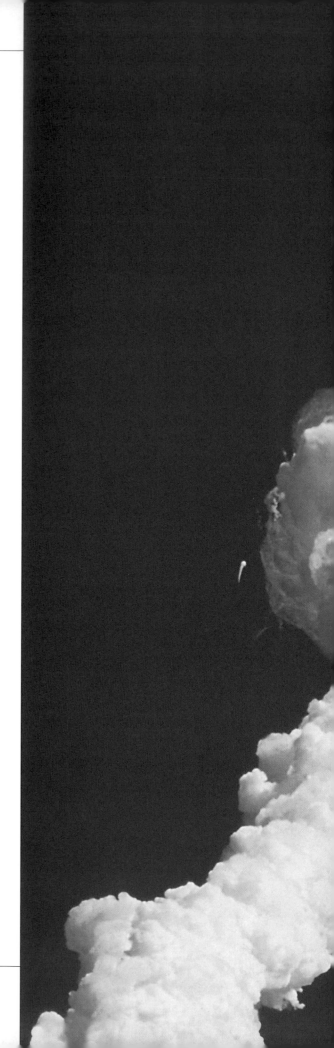

In the 16 years after Neil Armstrong walked on the Moon, Americans had made six more lunar trips and had orbited Earth for weeks at a time on Skylab. Many observers came to regard space travel as a routine affair. The 1981 introduction of the space shuttle, the world's first reusable space vehicle, only reinforced such a complacent view, especially after crews sometimes included nonastronauts like Christa McAuliffe, the high-school teacher aboard *Challenger* on January 28.

That complacency vanished when, 73 seconds after *Challenger* lifted off, burning gases escaping from a defective seal in one of its booster rockets touched off an explosion that destroyed the shuttle, killing all aboard. That night, President Reagan spoke to a grieving nation about *Challenger*'s heroes: "We will never forget them, nor the last time we saw them, this morning, as they . . . waved goodbye and 'slipped the surly bonds of earth' to 'touch the face of God.' "

The members of Challenger's crew were (clockwise from top left) Ellison S. Onizuka, Christa McAuliffe, Gregory Jarvis, Judith A. Resnik, Ronald E. McNair, Francis R. Scobee, and Michael J. Smith.

A total of 234 Pershing II missiles like this one were destroyed or disabled in accordance with the landmark 1987 INF Treaty.

1987
The INF Treaty

When Ronald Reagan, by far the most anti-Soviet American president of the nuclear age, called the Soviet Union the "evil empire" and the "focus of evil in the modern world" in March 1983, the Cold War seemed to enter one of its most frigid phases, and subsequent events only deepened the chill. In September, a Soviet fighter shot down a Korean Air jumbo jet, killing 269 passengers. The United States began deploying a new generation of nuclear-tipped ballistic and cruise missiles in Western Europe in December. And in 1984, the Soviets boycotted the summer Olympic Games, which were being held in the United States for the first time in 52 years.

Any chance that the prolonged tensions between the superpowers might lessen soon seemed remote. Then, in 1985, the Soviets gained a new, young leader, Mikhail Gorbachev. When he met with Reagan in Reykjavik, Iceland, in October 1986, he surprised the American delegation by expressing a willingness not just to reduce the number of nuclear missiles but to eliminate them altogether. The summit ended without a formal agreement and so was widely regarded as a failure, but Reagan himself called the meeting a "major turning point in the quest for a safe and secure world" because at it the leaders had laid the groundwork for one of the major milestones in the ending of the Cold War—the Intermediate-Range Nuclear Forces (INF) Treaty.

Signed in Washington, D.C., on December 8, 1987, the pact eliminated for the first time an entire class of atomic weapons—all ground-launched missiles capable of hitting targets between 300 and 3,400 miles away. It also laid out an unprecedented verification scheme that allowed inspectors from both countries to view the weapons' destruction. "Something extraordinary was taking place," *Time* magazine wrote of the cheerfulness that surrounded the signing. "Four decades of often truculent cold-war rhetoric were giving way to dispassionate discourse and high-level rapport."

Around the World

1989
Revolt in Tiananmen Square

The wave of reform rolling across Eastern Europe was one of the subjects Mikhail Gorbachev wanted to discuss with Chinese leader Deng Xiaoping when they met in China in May for the first official talks between their countries in 30 years. The historic summit was upstaged, however, when the wave reached China and generated the severest challenge to its leaders since the 1949 revolution (page 117). On May 13, 3,000 students gathered in Beijing's Tiananmen Square to demand political reform. Deng's economic reforms had boosted prosperity, but the protesters wanted much more, including Deng's resignation and the adoption of democratic principles. "We think everything must change," one young activist declared.

The demonstrations continued for weeks, swelling to one million participants. The atmosphere was more ebullient than desperate: Motorcyclists, acrobats, rock singers, a 33-foot repli-ca of the Statue of Liberty, and banners proclaiming "I Have a Dream" made the protest look like a street festival.

Hope turned to horror on May 20 when the government declared martial law. Crowds of citizens tried to halt the advance of the People's Liberation Army toward Tiananmen Square, but by June 3, troops and personnel carriers were less than a mile away. Before sunrise the next morning armored vehicles rolled into the square, crushing those who blocked their path. One column of tanks was stopped for six minutes by a single defiant youth (above) who became an icon of the revolution when his picture appeared in newspapers and magazines around the world. As many as 5,000 demonstrators were killed, and thousands more were arrested. Although the protest accelerated economic expansion, China resisted ideological reform, remaining a steadfastly Communist state at century's end.

Around the World

1989
The Fall of the Berlin Wall

For more than a generation the world knew no more imposing symbol of the Cold War than the Berlin Wall. Built in 1961 to halt the flight of East Germans to the West (page 128), the 28-mile-long barrier had filled its function with brutal efficiency. Yet in 1989, as reforms initiated by Soviet leader Mikhail Gorbachev shook the Soviet Union and Eastern Europe, cracks appeared in the Iron Curtain. Non-Communist governments came to power in Poland and Hungary. Protesters took to the streets in Leipzig and other East German cities. And Hungary opened its border with Austria, allowing hundreds of thousands of East Germans to cross over to the West.

Acknowledging that "the wheel of history" was turning faster, as West German chancellor Helmut Kohl put it, the leader of East Berlin's Communist Party on November 9 announced what had previously been unthinkable: Starting at midnight, East Germans would be free to leave their country.

Word of the policy spread quickly, and the mood turned festive. Berliners gathered on both sides of Checkpoint Charlie, the passageway through the wall, and chanted, "Tor auf!" ("Open the gate!") At the stroke of midnight, East German officials complied, and the world watched as thousands of jubilant East Germans streamed into the West. An observer described the event as a "combination of the fall of the Bastille and a New Year's Eve blowout, of revolution and celebration." West Berliners took hammers and chisels to the wall in the days that followed (above), then construction crews moved in to finish the job. Eleven months later, few traces of the hated barrier remained.

1990
Assisted Suicide

At the age of 54, Janet Adkins gave up. Experimental treatments that she and her family had hoped might reverse her Alzheimer's disease had failed; she was steadily losing her memory. Vowing to end her life before her condition worsened, she flew in June to Michigan and became the first person to use the suicide machine of pathologist Jack Kevorkian *(below)*, an advocate of physician-assisted suicide. In stark contrast to ubiquitous multimillion-dollar medical equipment designed to prolong life, his $45 device gave patients the means to stop their own hearts with the push of a button and placed him at the center of the charged debate about a doctor's role in euthanasia.

1990
Scandal on Wall Street

After suffering through recession in the '70s, the worst since the Depression, Wall Street in the '80s embarked on the greatest bull market in history. Fueled by lower interest rates, reduced inflation, and a wave of mergers and acquisitions, the boom enticed millions of investors into the market at the same time that it made celebrities of a cadre of bankers, raiders, and stock pickers.

Among the most famous were Ivan Boesky *(right, above)* and Michael Milken *(right, below)*. Boesky, a specialist in corporate takeovers, invested in companies that he surmised were about to be bought out, then sold the shares after the acquisition came to pass and the stock grew in value. By 1986 he had a fortune in excess of $200 million and a reputation as a stock-trading genius.

Milken, an executive with the Drexel Burnham Lambert investment firm, amassed his fortune in the market for high-risk, high-interest securities known as junk bonds. In 1984 he started selling the bonds to investors and lending the proceeds to corporate raiders, who used them to fund hostile takeovers.

But a change of fortune was in the offing. In May 1986 a federal investigation into insider trading netted a Drexel managing director who admitted sharing confidential information with Boesky. In December, Wall Street was jolted to learn that Boesky had negotiated a plea bargain, agreeing to a three-year prison term and penalties of $100 million. But the worst news was that he was cooperating with the government. "There'll be people named from almost every firm on Wall Street," fretted one banker.

Among them was Milken. Ensnared in what became the largest securities fraud case in U.S. history, he was indicted on 98 counts of racketeering and other crimes and in 1990 was sentenced to 10 years and fined $600 million—the heaviest ever levied against an individual. And, in the biggest Wall Street failure to date, Drexel Burnham Lambert collapsed, marking the end of a money-mad era.

Before his fall Boesky told University of California business-school graduates, "You can be greedy and still feel good about yourself."

Junk-bond guru Michael Milken earned $550 million in 1987, more than four times the profits of the investment firm he worked for.

1991
Desert Storm

Less than a year after the Berlin Wall fell, the United States faced its first crisis as the sole remaining superpower when on August 2, 1990, the forces of Iraqi dictator Saddam Hussein *(inset)* invaded Kuwait, a tiny country located north of the strategic oil fields of Saudi Arabia. The move put Iraq in a position to choke off much of the world's energy supply.

Vowing that such aggression "will not stand," American president George Bush put together a 28-nation military coalition to bolster Saudi defenses and persuaded the United Nations to impose economic sanctions on Iraq. Saddam, however, refused to withdraw his troops. At the end of November, the U.N. Security Council presented Saddam with an ultimatum: Either quit Kuwait by January 16 or face eviction by force. When the deadline passed, Desert Storm, the coalition's American-led attack, got under way with a spectacular aerial assault. CNN correspondent Bernard Shaw witnessed the raid from a hotel in Baghdad, Iraq's capital. "This feels like we're in the center of hell," he reported.

President George Bush tosses souvenir tie clips to troops in Saudi Arabia in November 1990, two months before Operation Desert Storm opened with the aerial assault on downtown Baghdad (right). Though spectacular to look at, the Iraqi antiaircraft fire crisscrossing the sky was largely ineffective.

A female American soldier cuddles her baby before shipping out to the Persian Gulf region. One of 41,000 women to serve in Desert Storm, she was part of the largest military deployment of women in American history.

Television viewers around the world sat transfixed as Shaw broadcast live while cruise missiles and radar-evading Stealth fighter planes—unseen but for the flash and smoke of their bombs—destroyed targets in the city and elsewhere. Hundreds more aircraft pressed the attack over the following weeks, pounding Iraqi positions in advance of what Saddam promised would be the "mother of all battles." Yet when the coalition kicked off its long-awaited ground assault on February 24, his soldiers failed to live up to the rhetoric. Weakened by the air campaign and facing an opponent of overwhelming superiority, many Iraqis quickly surrendered. Others ran. Of those who fought, most were killed. By February 27, only 100 hours after the beginning of the ground war, Kuwait had been liberated, and President Bush announced that he was suspending all offensive action.

"We went halfway around the world to do what is moral and just and right," he later told Congress. "We lifted the yoke of aggression and tyranny from a small country that many Americans had never even heard of, and we asked nothing in return. We're coming home now proud, confident, heads high."

The navy jet at left was part of the armada of bombers, fighters, and other aircraft that crushed the Iraqi military. Many carried not only "smart bombs," which could be guided toward their targets with unheard-of precision, but also video cameras, which allowed the TV audience to watch the bombs' devastating effects

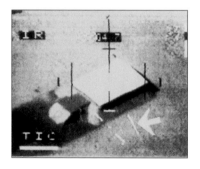
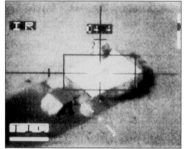
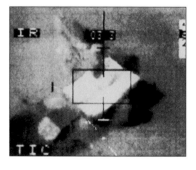
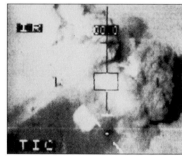

"It's easy to get lost out here. There are no terrain features. It's like the Kmart parking lot."

A scout for the 82nd Airborne Division in northern Saudi Arabia

Desert Storm commander General H. Norman Schwarzkopf points to a map of Iraq during a briefing for journalists on February 27, the eve of the cease-fire. He designed the winning strategy used in the Gulf War two years before the Iraqis invaded Kuwait.

Joint Chiefs of Staff chairman Colin Powell said of the Iraqi army, "First we're going to cut it off, and then we're going to kill it."

Marines wearing gas masks take aim with an automatic weapon near Kuwait's airport soon after the opening of the ground attack.

1992
The New Americans

History repeated itself between 1983 and 1992, when almost 8.7 million immigrants arrived on the nation's shores. This number was the highest in any decade since the years between 1900 and 1910, when nearly nine million newcomers arrived *(pages 46-47),* and it marked a high point of the century's second great wave of immigration.

The century's first wave became a trickle after 1924, when Congress set an annual limit of 150,000 immigrants and assigned quotas by country. These quotas reflected the prejudice of Americans with roots in northern and western Europe against immigrants from other places. Countries in southern and eastern Europe, which had supplied huge numbers of immigrants since the turn of the century, were allotted a total of only 16 percent of the quotas. By contrast, 82 percent were reserved for northern and western Europe. That left only 2 percent for all the other countries in the world.

At President Lyndon Johnson's urging, this so-called national-origins quota system was abolished in 1965. New policies were far more inclusive, and the wave of immigration that followed had a brand-new look. In 1978, for example, half of the arrivals were from Asia, and about one in four came from Central and South America. Only one in 10 was a European. New Americans like the young man shown above at a 1991 naturalization ceremony reminded everyone that this nation is, in the words of *Time* magazine's Robert Hughes, "a construction of mind, not of race or inherited class or ancestral territory. . . . America is a collective act of the imagination whose making never ends."

1993
The Web

For its first 20 years, the Internet was a globe-circling network of supercomputers run by experts versed in arcane codes at universities and other big institutions. In 1990 a new system for linking sites on the Internet, the World Wide Web, did away with such codes, but people who didn't have access to a supercomputer couldn't use it. Then, in 1993, programmers at the University of Illinois released Mosaic, the first software that put the Web within reach of virtually every computer. Commercial programs based on Mosaic soon appeared, and millions of ordinary people started surfing the Web to check the weather in Kuala Lumpur or get advice on binoculars for birders.

"On the Internet, nobody knows you're a dog."

1993
Baby Boomers
Take Charge

When 46-year-old Bill Clinton became president on January 20, the baby boom generation—the 72 million Americans born between 1947 and 1964 *(pages 114-115)* —officially came of age. Clinton's election mirrored his contemporaries' rise to power in all segments of society as the generation that fought World War II passed the torch to the first generation born in its aftermath.

While many Americans welcomed the change, Clinton's inauguration came as something of a shock to his fellow boomers. As one of them said, "Instead of being able to feel like we're still kids and having to look up at the generation running things, suddenly there's a guy your age who is President of the United States."

> "There is nothing wrong with America that cannot be cured by what is right with America. . . . To renew America, we . . . must do what no generation has had to do before."
>
> Bill Clinton, inaugural address

President-elect Bill Clinton and running mate Al Gore clasp hands with their wives as they greet supporters in Little Rock, Arkansas, on election night in 1992. Clinton became the third-youngest president in history

1993
The Hubble Telescope

Grounded for 32 months after the *Challenger* explosion *(pages 168-169)*, the nation's three remaining shuttles roared back into space in 1988, starting work on a long list of scientific and military missions. *Atlantis* launched probes destined for Venus and Jupiter. *Columbia* placed a communications satellite in orbit and set a record for the longest shuttle mission to date. And *Discovery* in April 1990 launched the $1.6 billion Hubble Space Telescope, whose ultimate mission is to gauge the age of the universe.

A bus-size satellite crammed with cameras, communications gear, and a main mirror nearly eight feet in diameter, Hubble promised what *Time* called "a leap in astronomical observing power unlike anything since 1609, when Galileo first pointed a telescope at the heavens." Yet when optics experts studied its first pictures, they were shocked to see signs of a flaw in the main mirror. The discovery embarrassed NASA officials, who were still struggling with the implications of the *Challenger* disaster. But the agency salvaged its reputation at the end of 1993, when astronauts aboard *Endeavour*—the shuttle built to replace *Challenger*—captured the telescope as it orbited 380 miles above the Earth, anchored it in the shuttle's payload bay, and, in a record-making five spacewalks, repaired it *(inset)*.

It was the most complicated shuttle mission ever. Hubble has performed flawlessly since, sending spectacular images of never-before-seen stars and galaxies such as the Eagle Nebula, seen at left.

1994
Gay Rights

Police raids on gay bars in Greenwich Village had for years been routine affairs that concluded with the arrest of a few patrons. But the officers who raided the Stonewall Inn on June 28, 1969, were in for a shock: Sick of such harassment, the patrons resisted and rioted. For gay and lesbian Americans, the uprising came to mark the beginning of a movement that fought discrimination and brought them into the country's mainstream. To celebrate the movement's accomplishments and commemorate Stonewall's 25th anniversary, marchers in 1994 staged a parade, during which the milelong rainbow banner below rippled through Manhattan as a symbol of unity.

Around the World

1994
A New Day for South Africa

In 1964 Nelson Mandela told a South African court about his dream of "a democratic and free society in which all persons live together in harmony and with equal opportunities." Unpersuaded, the court sentenced him to life in prison for trying to sabotage the white minority government. From behind bars Mandela continued to wage a tireless campaign against the repressive regime. A 300-year tradition of racial segregation had become codified as law in 1948 after the Nationalist Party rose to power on a platform of apartheid (literally, "separateness"). Most of South Africa's 30 million blacks were forced into rural homelands or townships on the fringes of urban areas. Unable to travel freely in white areas, they lived in abject poverty, without electricity, running water, or an adequate educational system, and anyone who resisted apartheid risked imprisonment or death.

But antiapartheid pressure from inside and outside South Africa mounted, and in 1990 the newly elected president, F. W. de Klerk, responded to it dramatically: He released Mandela from prison and began to dismantle apartheid. De Klerk's program of "evolutionary reform" climaxed in 1994 with the unthinkable: For the first time, blacks were permitted to vote in all-race elections. The 75-year-old Mandela (above) was swept to victory as president and, 30 years after his conviction, could begin to realize his dream of a new South Africa. Democracy brought no guarantee of harmony in a land that still bore the scars of savage inequality, brutality, and racial persecution. But a hopeful Mandela told his countrymen, "Let there be justice for all. Let their be work, bread and salt for all. The time for the healing of the wounds has come."

1995
Global Warming

As long ago as 1898 a Swedish scientist named Svante Ahrrenius raised the possibility that carbon dioxide released by factories burning coal and oil was accumulating in the atmosphere. If that was true, the rising carbon dioxide level could intensify the atmosphere's natural greenhouse effect, letting in sunlight but preventing more and more of the resulting heat from radiating back into space. Over time, the Earth's temperature would rise.

In 1995 the Intergovernmental Panel on Climate Change (IPCC), a U.N.-sponsored body of 2,500 climatologists from 60 nations, issued a definitive report on global warming. It declared that the evidence was conclusive: Because of human activity, the world's climate was changing. Although skeptics charged that the dangers were overstated, the IPCC forecast "widespread economic, social and environmental dislocation" unless the world took swift measures to reduce emissions of not only carbon dioxide but also other gases such as methane. Experts predicted that the average global temperature would rise between two and six degrees Fahrenheit by the year 2100. As glaciers melted, sea levels might rise as much as three feet, inundating heavily populated coastlines and islands. Animal populations would die out as their ecosystems were destroyed, and changing patterns of rainfall and snow would bring protracted crop-destroying droughts to some regions, while others would suffer heavy rainfall and flooding, as shown in the 1996 photo below of a farm near the Mississippi River.

The evidence of global warming has led several nations to propose new standards for reducing greenhouse gas emissions. But such regulations are no guarantee of a climatically stable future. "We're conducting a global experiment," commented a Stanford University biologist. "And we're all in the test tube."

1997
Cloning

From Mary Shelley's Frankenstein to H. G. Wells's The Island of Dr. Moreau, creating new beings out of adult body parts has been the stuff of science fiction. Fiction became fact in 1997 when scientists in Roslin, Scotland, announced that they had cloned a lamb named Dolly (above) from a cell taken from the udder of a fully grown sheep.

Dolly presented humans with the tantalizing but unnerving prospect that they might someday be able to produce copies of themselves. Dr. Ian Wilmut, Dolly's creator, acknowledged that in theory his method could be used to clone people but hastened to add, "I would find it offensive." Instead he stressed the potential for enormous medical benefits. Biologists could genetically alter cells to produce drugs, such as a blood-clotting agent for treating hemophilia, and then clone the cells to create animals who would make the drug in their milk. Species on the brink of extinction could also be cloned. Faced with the most portentous scientific discovery since the atom bomb (pages 110-111), humanity struggled with the implications of its brave new world.

1997
Trailblazing on Mars

On July 4 the Mars lander *Pathfinder* bounced to a stop, and soon astonishingly sharp color photos of the planet's landscape were reaching Earth. Called the Ares Vallis, the landing site was thickly strewn with rocks deposited a billion or more years ago in massive flooding. Scientists had picked the site in hopes that the debris had been swept from many different places and would provide a rich geological sampling—and, possibly, signs of ancient life.

 Pathfinder's camera, mounted on a mast extending 1.8 meters above the one-meter-high landing craft, captured the panorama *(right)*. A robot, *Sojourner,* rolled down a ramp from the mother ship and roamed the surface shooting closeups with three cameras. In addition, the robot's spectrometer analyzed gas and mineral samples to determine how the resources of Earth's closest planetary neighbor can be used by humans when they set foot there one day.

Skateboard-size robot Sojourner (right) perches atop Mars lander Pathfinder shortly after landing on the planet's surface.

ACKNOWLEDGMENTS

The editors wish to thank the following individuals and institutions:
Alexandria Police Department, Alexandria, Va.; Richard Allen, Lynden, Wash.; American Cancer Society, Atlanta; American Federation of Police, Miami, Fla.; Judy and Ed Ashley, Jed Collectibles, Pemberton, N.J.; David Burgoven, Smithsonian Institution, Washington, D.C.; Robert L. D. Colby, Securities and Exchange Commission, Washington, D.C.; Matthew Cook, Chicago Historical Society, Chicago; Duery Felton Jr., Vietnam Veterans Memorial Collection, National Park Service, Glenn Dale, Md.; Mike Gentry, NASA Media Services, Houston, Tex.; Cyndy Gilley, Do You Graphics, Woodbine, Md.; Robert Hornak, Star Wars Collectibles, Alexandria, Va.; Dr. William Kincade, American University School of International Service, Washington, D.C.; Jay Klehfoth, Model T Ford Club of America, Dallas; Eric T. L. Love, University of Kansas, Lawrence; Antony Porco, Vietnam Veterans Memorial Collection, National Park Service, Glenn Dale, Md.; Kathleen Ryan, Philadelphia Museum of Art, Philadelphia; Milo Stewart Jr., National Baseball Hall of Fame and Museum; Cooperstown, N.Y.; George Theofiles, "Miscellaneous Man," New Freedom, Pa.; Tom Way, IBM Corporation, Essex Junction, Vt.

PICTURE CREDITS

The sources for the illustrations in this book appear below. Credits from left to right are separated by semicolons; credits from top to bottom are separated by dashes.

Cover and dust jacket: Corbis-Bettmann; Culver Pictures Inc., New York; Corbis-Bettmann; U.S. Army; AP/Wide World Photos; © 1995 Elliott Erwitt/Magnum Photos Inc., New York; photograph by © Harris & Ewing, collection of the Supreme Court of the United States—National Aeronautics and Space Administration (NASA).
3: Alfred Eisenstaedt, *Life* Magazine © Time Inc. 6, 7: NASA. 8, 9: Chicago Historical Society (ICHi-04191). 10, 11: Movie Still Archives, Harrison, Nebr. 12, 13: UPI/Corbis-Bettmann. 14, 15: Photo by Dorothea Lange, Library of Congress USZ-62-118228. 16, 17: Library of Congress USZ-62-45642. 18, 19: UPI/Corbis-Bettmann. 20, 21: Hy Peskin, *Life* Magazine © Time Inc. 22, 23: Charles Moore/Black Star, New York. 24, 25: Larry Burrows, *Life* Magazine © Time Inc.. 26, 27: NASA. 28: Corbis-Bettmann. 29: SuperStock, Inc., Jacksonville, Fla. 30: Photograph by Tom Way, courtesy IBM Corporation. 31: © Les Stone/SYGMA, New York. 32: Stock Imagery, Denver, Colo. 33: Library of Congress from *Field to Factory: Afro-American Migration 1915-1940* by Spencer R. Crew, ©1987 Smithsonian Institution, Washington, D.C. 34: John Olson, *Life* Magazine © Time Inc. 35: John Biever/*Sports Illustrated*. 36: National Park Service, Statue of Liberty National Monument. 38: State Historical Society of Wisconsin, WHi D28 85—The Huntington Library and Art Gallery, San Marino, Calif.—Fischer Collection, State Historical Society of Wisconsin, WHi F5 5 19—George Eastman House, Rochester, N.Y., photos by Barbara Purro Galasso (2). 39: Carnegie Library of Pittsburgh, file no. C-1062—Culver Pictures Inc., New York—Carnegie Library of Pittsburgh, neg. no. A-146. 40: Milo Stewart Jr./National Baseball Hall of Fame Library, Cooperstown, N.Y. (2)—courtesy Boston Public Library, Boston. 41: National Baseball Hall of Fame Library, Cooperstown, N.Y. 42, 43: Archives and Special Collections, University Library, Wright State University, Dayton, Ohio, except top right, Library of Congress. 44, 45: J. B. Monaco Photo; courtesy Richard Monaco, San Francisco: Jed Collectibles, Pemberton, N.J. 46: Photography by Karen Yamauchi for Chermayeff & Geismar Inc./MetaForm Inc. 47: Library of Congress, photo by Edwin Levick, USZ-62-1120. 48: Lewis B. Hine, New York Public Library, Special Collections, Astor, Lenox and Tilden Foundations. 49: Photography by Karen Yamauchi for Chermayeff & Geismar Inc./MetaForm Inc. 50: Corbis-Bettmann; Brown Brothers, Sterling, Pa. 51: Corbis-Bettmann. 52, 53: Hirshhorn Museum and Sculpture Garden, Smithsonian Institution, Elmer Mac Rae papers. Gift of Joseph H. Hirshhorn, 1966—The Baltimore Museum of Art: The Cone Collection, formed by Dr. Claribel Cone and Miss Etta Cone of Baltimore, Maryland BMA 1950.228; Constantin Brancusi, *Mlle. Pogany*, Philadelphia Museum of Art, given by Mrs. Rodolphe Meyer de Schauensee, photo by Graydon Wood, 1994—Philadelphia Museum of Art: The Louise and Walter Arensberg Collection. 54, 55: From the Collections of Henry Ford Museum and Greenfield Village, Dearborn, Mich. (2); courtesy Kruse International, Auburn, Ind. 56: Roger-Viollet, Paris; MOMA Film Stills Archive, New York. 57: Hershenson-Allen Archive, West Plains, Mo.—Photofest, New York; courtesy Piggly Wiggly Company, Memphis, Tenn. 58, 59: Library of Congress USZ-262-12880; Library of Congress USZ-262-12876. 60: Armed Forces Collections, Archive Center, National Museum of American History, Washington, D.C.—National Archives, War and Conflict 460: 61: National Archives, 111-SC-4052. 62, 63: National Archives, War and Conflict 644; Armed Forces Collections, Archive Center, National Museum of American History, Smithsonian Institution, Washington, D.C., photo by Fil Hunter—National Archives, War and Conflict 668. 64, 65: Courtesy Harris Andrews; FPG International, New York; National Archives 111-SC-62979. 66: Courtesy Barry Halper, photos by Henry Groskinsky; except top right, National Baseball Hall of Fame Library, Cooperstown, N.Y. 67: From *Our Times: The Illustrated History of the 20th Century*, editor in chief, Lorraine Glennon, Turner Publishing, Inc. 1995—Culver Pictures, Inc., New York. 68, 69: UPI/Corbis-Bettmann; AP/Wide World Photos—UPI/Corbis-Bettmann. 70: Sophia Smith Collection, Smith College, Northampton, Mass. (2)—Library of Congress H261-9798. 71: Library of Congress USZ-62-095442. 72: Waves Inc., New York—courtesy Miss America Organization. 73: Archive Photos, New York. 74, 75: Corbis-Bettmann; Deans Foods Vegetable Co., courtesy *Frozen Food Age*. 76: Hulton Getty Picture Collection, London—Stanley Apfelbaum. 77: UPI/Corbis-Bettmann. 78: © Disney Enterprises, Inc.; The Kobal Collection, London; Corbis-Bettmann. 79: UPI/Corbis-Bettmann. 80, 81: George Eastman House, Rochester, N.Y., neg. no. 36707. 82: Corbis-Bettmann. 83: Photo of White Angel Breadline, San Francisco (detail), copyright the Dorothea Lange Collection, Oakland Museum of California, The City of Oakland, gift of Paul S. Taylor, neg. no. 8010325. 84, 85: AP/Wide World Photos. 86: Bundesarchiv, Koblenz. 87: UPI/Corbis-Bettmann—Library of Congress. 88: Photo of Family on the Road, Midwest (detail), copyright the Dorothea Lange Collection, Oakland Museum, The City of Oakland, gift of Paul S. Taylor, neg. no. 67.137.38239.2. 89: Corbis-Bettmann. 90: Hake's Americana & Collectibles, York, Pa.; UPI/Corbis-Bettmann. 91: Corbis-Bettmann. 92: Library of Congress USZC4-4890. 93: AP/Wide World Photos. 94: UPI/Corbis-Bettmann. 95: Movie Still Archives, Harrison, Nebr. 96, 97: Popperfoto, Overstone, North Hamptonshire, U.K.; Library of Congress, from *Danzig* by Carl Otto Windecker; © 1941 Schutzen-Verlag GmbH, Berlin SW68; CAF Photo Archives, Warsaw. 98, 99: USS *Arizona* Memorial, Hawaii, photo by Henry Groskinsky; National Archives 080-G-19942. 100, 101: AP/Wide World Photos; National Archives, 210-6A-35; National Archives. 102: Frank Scherschel, *Life* Magazine © Time Inc.. 103: AP/Wide World Photos. 104: U.S. Army. 105: U.S. Army; UPI/Corbis-Bettmann. 106, 107: Louis R. Lowery/U.S. Marine Corps. 108, 109: Margaret Bourke-White. 110: UPI/Corbis-Bettmann—Brian Brake/Photo Researchers. 111: U.S. Air Force photo. 112, 113: UPI/Corbis-Bettmann. 114, 115: Photo © 1998 Time Life Inc.; Bernard Hoffman, *Life* Magazine © Time Inc.; Archive Photos, New York; courtesy Patricia and Allen Ahearn, Quill & Brush, Rockville, Md.—courtesy Bought Again Books, Cedar Falls, Iowa. 116: © 1948 Time Inc. Reprinted by permission—Walter Sanders, *Life* Magazine © Time Inc. 117: Courtesy Professor Clifton Olds, Bowdoin College, Brunswick, Maine; courtesy Diners Club International. 118, 119: David Douglas Duncan, *Life* Magazine © Time Inc. 120: Hank Walker, *Life* Magazine © Time Inc.; Ed Clark, *Life* Magazine © Time Inc. 121: Michael Beasley, courtesy Zenith Corporation, Glenview, Ill., inset photo, Photofest, New York; courtesy March of Dimes. 122, 123: Carl Iwasaki, *Life* Magazine © Time Inc.—photograph by Fabian Bachrach, collection of the Supreme Court of the United States; AP/Wide World Photos. 124: Courtesy McDonald's Corp., Oak Brook, Ill.; courtesy Missouri Department of Transportation. 125: Michael Ochs Archives, Venice, Calif.; courtesy Jeanne R. Jackson—Charles Trainor. 126: George Silk, *Life* Magazine © Time Inc.—© 1957 Burt Glinn/Magnum Photos, Inc. New York. 127: Dmitri Kessel, *Life* Magazine © Time Inc.—Novosti from Sovfoto/Eastfoto, New York; courtesy G. D. Searle & Co., Chicago. 128: Hake's Americana & Collectibles, York, Pa. (2); Peter Leibing/Conti-Press for AP/Wide World Photos—AP/Wide World Photos. 129: Photri Inc., Falls Church, Va. 130, 131: Courtesy Thomas C. Whiteford; Seymour Raskin/Magnum Photos, Inc., New York; courtesy Nancy Finken. 132: © 1963 Fred Ward/Black Star, New York—UPI/Corbis-Bettmann. 133: © 1963 Fred Ward/Black Star, New York, inset photo © 1963 Steve Schapiro/Black Star, New York. 134: Art Rickerby, *Life* Magazine © Time Inc. 135: Abraham Zapruder, © Time Inc. (4); Cecil W. Stoughton—Bob Jackson. 136, 137: UPI/Corbis-Bettmann (2); © 1995 Elliott Erwitt/Magnum Photos Inc., New York. 138: Courtesy Antonio Alcalá; Corbis-Bettmann. 140: Photograph by Larry Burrows, © Larry Burrows Collection. 141: Tim Page. 142, 143: © James H. Karales/Peter Arnold, Inc., New York. 144: Courtesy National Association of Chiefs of Police © 1998. All rights reserved. 145: Walter Iooss/*Sports Illus-*

BIBLIOGRAPHY

BOOKS

Adams, John G. *Without Precedent.* New York: W. W. Norton, 1983.

Adams, Robert McCormick. *Paths of Fire.* Princeton, N.J.: Princeton University Press, 1996.

Albert, Judith Clavir, and Stewart Edward Albert. *The Sixties Papers.* New York: Praeger, 1984.

Allen, Frederick Lewis:
  The Big Change. New York: Harper & Row, 1952.
  Only Yesterday. New York: Perennial Library, 1931.

The Almanac of American History. Ed. by Arthur M. Schlesinger, Jr. New York: G. P. Putnam's Sons, 1983.

Ambrose, Stephen E.:
  D-Day, June 6, 1944. New York: Simon & Schuster, 1994.
  Eisenhower (Vol. 2). New York. Simon & Schuster, 1984.

American Decades (selected volumes, 1920-1979). Detroit: Gale Research, 1995 1997.

Bell, Daniel. *The Cultural Contradictions of Capitalism.* New York: Basic Books, 1978.

Bergreen, Laurence. *Capone.* New York: Simon & Schuster, 1994.

Beschloss, Michael R. *The Crisis Years.* New York: Edward Burlingame Books, 1991.

Boorstin, Daniel J. *The Americans.* New York: Vintage Books, 1973.

Bordley, James, III. *Two Centuries of American Medicine: 1776 1976.* Philadelphia: W. B. Saunders, 1976.

Bowman, John. *Andrew Carnegie: Steel Tycoon.* Englewood Cliffs, N.J.: Silver Burdett Press, 1989.

Bridges, Herb, and Terryl C. Boodman. *Gone With the Wind.* New York: Simon & Schuster, 1989.

Brody, David. *Workers in Industrial America: Essays on the Twentieth Century Struggle.* New York: Oxford University Press, 1993.

Brooks, Tim, and Earle Marsh. *The Complete Directory to Prime Time Network TV Shows: 1946-Present.* New York: Ballantine Books, 1988.

Brown, Milton Wolf. *The Story of the Armory Show.* New York: Abbeville Press, 1988.

Brugioni, Dino A. *Eyeball to Eyeball.* New York: Random House, 1991.

Chafe, William H. *The Unfinished Journey: America Since World War II.* New York: Oxford University Press, 1986.

Chermayeff, Ivan. *Ellis Island.* New York: Macmillan, 1991.

Chronicle of America. New York: DK Publishing, 1997.

Chronicle of the 20th Century. London: Dorling Kindersley, 1995.

Coe, Brian. *Kodak Cameras: The First Hundred Years.* Hove, East Sussex, U.K.: Hove Foto Books, 1988.

Corey, Lewis. *The House of Morgan.* New York: G. Howard Watt, 1930.

Cowan, Ruth Schwartz. *A Social History of American Technology.* New York: Oxford University Press, 1997.

Daniels, Roger. *Prisoners Without Trial.* New York: Hill and Wang, 1993.

Denenberg, Barry. *The True Story of J. Edgar Hoover and the FBI.* New York: Scholastic, 1993.

Dickson, Paul. *The Great American Ice Cream Book.* New York: Atheneum, 1973.

Duden, Jane. *1950s.* New York: Crestwood House, 1989.

Ellis, Edward Robb. *Echoes of Distant Thunder: Life in the United States, 1914-1918.* New York: Kodansha International, 1996.

Encyclopedia of the American Presidency (Vols. 1, 2, and 3). Ed. by Leonard W. Levy and Louis Fisher. New York: Simon & Schuster, 1994.

Events: A Chronicle of the Twentieth Century. Ed. by Philip L. Cottrell. Oxford: Oxford University Press, 1992.

Ewald, William Bragg, Jr. *Who Killed Joe McCarthy?* New York: Simon & Schuster, 1984.

Faber, John. *Great News Photos and the Stories Behind Them.* New York: Dover, 1978.

Facts on File Yearbook (selected volumes, 1960-1973). York: Facts on File, 1961-1974.

Ferrell, Robert H., and Richard Natkiel. *Atlas of American History.* New York: Facts on File, 1987.

Fischer, Daniel, and Hilmar Duerbeck. *Hubble.* Trans. by Helmut Jenkner and Douglas Duncan. New York: Copernicus, 1996.

Freedman, Russell:
  Kids at Work. New York: Clarion Books, 1994.
  The Wright Brothers. New York: Holiday House, 1991.

Gadney, Reg. *Kennedy.* New York: Holt, Rinehart and Winston, 1983.

Garrow, David J. *Bearing the Cross.* New York: William Morrow, 1986.

Gay, Peter. *Freud: A Life for Our Time.* New York: W. W. Norton, 1988.

Glassman, Bruce. *The Crash of '29 and the New Deal.* Morristown, N.J.: Silver Burdett, 1986.

Goodwin, Doris Kearns. *No Ordinary Time.* New York: Touchstone, 1994.

Gordon, Lois, and Alan Gordon. *American Chronicle.* New York: Crown Publishers, 1990.

Green, Harvey. *The Uncertainty of Everyday Life, 1915-1945.* New York: Harper-Collins, 1992.

Guralnick, Peter. *Last Train to Memphis.* Boston: Little, Brown, 1994.

Guynes, David. "The Importance of the Collection." In *The Last Firebase,* ed. by Lydia Fish. Shippensburg, Pa.: White Mane, 1987.

Halberstam, David. *The Fifties.* New York: Fawcett Columbine, 1993.

Hale, Nathan G. *Freud and the Americans.* New York: Oxford University Press, 1971.

Hine, Lewis W. *Men at Work.* New York: Dover Publications, 1977.

A History of the African American People. New York: Smithmark, 1995.

Hofstadter, Richard. *The Age of Reform.* New York: Vintage Books, 1955.

Hornsby, Alton, Jr. *Milestones in 20th-Century African-American History.* Detroit: Visible Ink Press, 1993.

Ingraham, Gloria D., and Leonard W. Ingraham. *An Album of American Women: Their Changing Role.* New York: Franklin Watts, 1987.

Jones, James H. *Alfred C. Kinsey.* New York: W. W. Norton, 1997.

Kasher, Steven. *The Civil Rights Movement.* New York: Abbeville Press, 1996.

Kent, Zachary. *The Story of the Challenger Disaster.* Chicago: Childrens Press, 1986.

Kerrod, Robin. *The Illustrated History of NASA.* London: Multimedia, 1986.

Kinsey, Alfred C., Wardell B. Pomeroy, and Clyde E. Martin. *Sexual Behavior in the Human Male.* Philadelphia: W. B. Saunders, 1948.

Lemann, Nicholas. *The Promised Land: The Great Black Migration and How It Changed America.* New York: Vintage Books, 1991.

Life in Camelot. Ed. by Philip B. Kunhardt, Jr. Boston: Little, Brown, 1988.

Life—the '60s. Ed. by Doris C. O'Neil, Jr. Boston: Little, Brown, 1989.

Lord, Walter. *The Good Years: From 1900 to the First World War.* New York: Harper & Brothers, 1960.

McCall, Michael. *The Best of 50s TV.* New York: Mallard Press, 1992.

McCullough, David. *Mornings on Horseback.* New York: Simon & Schuster, 1981.

McGowen, Tom. *World War II.* New York: Franklin Watts, 1993.

Makower, Joel. *Woodstock.* New York: Doubleday, 1989.

Marling, Karal Ann. *As Seen on TV.* Cambridge, Mass.: Harvard University Press, 1994.

Marshall, S. L. A. *American Heritage History of World War I.* New York: American Heritage, 1982.

Martin Luther King, Jr.: A Documentary . . . Montgomery to Memphis. New York: W. W. Norton, 1976.

Miller, Douglas T., and Marion Nowak. *The Fifties: The Way We Really Were.* Garden City, N.Y.: Doubleday, 1977.

Morgan, Edward P. *The 60s Experience: Hard Lessons About Modern America.* Philadelphia: Temple University Press, 1991.

Morris, Edmund. *The Rise of Theodore Roosevelt.* New York: Coward, McCann & Geoghegan, 1979.

Nevins, Allan. *Ford: The Times, the Man, the Company.* New York: Charles Scribner's Sons, 1954.

Oakley, J. Ronald. *God's Country: America in the Fifties.* New York: Dembner Books, 1986.

Our Glorious Century. Pleasantville, N. Y.: Reader's Digest, 1994.

Our Times: The Illustrated History of the 20th Century. Atlanta: Turner Publishing, 1995.

The Oxford Companion to World War II. Oxford: Oxford University Press, 1995.

Pach, Chester J., Jr., and Elmo Richardson. *The Presidency of Dwight D. Eisenhower.* Lawrence: University Press of Kansas, 1991.

Palladino, Grace. *Teenagers.* New York: BasicBooks, 1996.

Patterson, James T. *Grand Expectations: The United States, 1945-1974.* New York: Oxford University Press, 1996.

Phillips, Louis, and Burnham Holmes. *The TV Almanac.* New York: Macmillan, 1994.

Players of Cooperstown. Lincolnwood, Ill.: Publications International, 1992.

Reader's Companion to American History. Ed. by Eric Foner and John A. Garraty. Boston: Houghton Mifflin, 1991.

Rhoads, B. Eric. *Blast From the Past.* West Palm Beach, Fla.: Streamline Press, 1996.

Ritter, Lawrence S.:
The Babe: A Life in Pictures. New York: Ticknor & Fields, 1988.
The Glory of Their Times. New York: Macmillan, 1966.

The Rolling Stone Illustrated History of Rock and Roll. Ed. by Anthony DeCurtis, James Henke, and Holly George-Warren. New York: Random House, 1992.

Schickel, Richard. *D. W. Griffith:.* New York: Simon & Schuster, 1984.

Schlesinger, Arthur M., Jr. *The Coming of the New Deal.* Boston: Houghton Mifflin, 1959.

The Settling of North America.. Ed. by Helen Hornbeck Tanner. New York: Macmillan, 1995.

Sinclair, Upton. *The Jungle.* New York: Bantam Books, 1981.

Smith, Nigel. *The United States Since 1945.* New York: Bookwright Press, 1990.

Stein, Leon. *The Triangle Fire.* Philadelphia: J. B. Lippincott, 1962.

Stein, R. Conrad. *The Story of the San Francisco Earthquake.* Chicago: Childrens Press, 1983.

Strauss, William. *Generations: The History of America's Future, 1584 to 2069.* New York: William Morrow, 1991.

Sulzberger, C. L.:
The American Heritage Picture History of World War II. New York: Wings Books, 1995.
World War II. New York: American Heritage, 1985.

Susman, Warren I. *Culture as History.* New York: Pantheon Books, 1984.

Tauranac, John. *The Empire State Building:.* New York: Scribner, 1995.

Teweles, Richard J., and Edward S. Bradley. *The Stock Market.* New York: John Wiley & Sons, 1987.

Thomas, Gordon, and Max Morgan Witts. *The San Francisco Earthquake.* New York: Stein and Day, 1971.

Trager, James. *The People's Chronology.* New York: Henry Holt, 1992.

Turner, Henry Ashby, Jr. *Hitler's Thirty Days to Power: January 1933.* Reading, Mass.: Addison-Wesley, 1996.

Ungar, Sanford J. *Fresh Blood.* New York: Simon & Schuster, 1995.

U.S. Bureau of the Census:
Historical Statistics of the United States: Colonial Times to 1970 (parts 1 and 2). Washington, D.C.: U.S. Bureau of the Census, 1975.
Statistical Abstract of the United States (2 vols., 1995 and 1996). Washington, D.C.: U.S. Bureau of the Census, 1995, 1996.

U.S. Department of Education. *Digest of Education Statistics, 1996.* Washington, D.C.: U. S. Department of Education, 1997.

Wallace, James. *Overdrive: Bill Gates and the Race to Control Cyberspace.* New York: John Wiley & Sons, 1997.

Walton, George. *Twelve Events That Changed Our World.* New York: Cowles Book Co., 1970.

Ward, Geoffrey C. *Baseball.* New York: Alfred A. Knopf, 1994.

Watkins, T. H. *The Great Depression.* Boston: Little, Brown, 1993.

The Way We Were. Ed. by Robert MacNeil. New York: Carroll & Graf Publishers, 1988.

We Americans. Washington, D.C.: National Geographic Society, 1988.

Welsh, Douglas. *The USA in World War 2: The Pacific Theater.* New York: Galahad Books, 1982.

Wexler, Sanford. *The Civil Rights Movement.* New York: Facts on File, 1993.

Williams, Trevor. *Science.* Oxford: Oxford University Press, 1990.

Winter, Jay, and Blaine Baggett. *The Great War and the Shaping of the 20th Century.* New York: Penguin Studio, 1996.

Woodward, Bob, and Carl Bernstein. *The Final Days.* New York: Simon & Schuster, 1976.

The World's Great News Photos, 1840-1980. Ed. by Craig T. Norback and Melvin Gray. New York: Crown, 1980.

Wright, Orville. *How We Invented the Airplane.* New York: Dover, 1988.

PERIODICALS

"The Age of Cloning." *Time,* Mar. 10, 1997.

Anderson, Kurt. "A Homecoming at Last." *Time,* Nov. 22, 1982.

"As Hamburgers Go, So Goes America?" *Economist,* Aug. 23, 1997.

Barone, Michael. "A Century of Renewal." *U.S. News & World Report,* Aug. 28-Sept. 4, 1995.

Barrett, Craig R. "From Sand to Silicon: Manufacturing an Integrated Circuit." *Scientific American,* Nov. 1997.

Begley, Sharon:
"Pathfinder: The Stars of Mars." *Newsweek,* July 21, 1997.
"Space: NASA's Mr. and Ms. Goodwrench Fix the Hubble Telescope." *Newsweek,* Dec. 20, 1993.

Carson, Gerald. "The Income Tax and How It Grew." *American Heritage,* Dec. 1973.

Clark, Ronald W. "Sigmund Freud's Sortie to America." *American Heritage,* April/May 1980.

"Closing In on Polio." *Time,* Mar. 29, 1954.

"Doubts About Immigration." *Economist,* Sept. 27, 1997.

Etzioni, Amitai. "A Look at Racial Identity: Let's Not Be Boxed In by Color." *Washington Post,* June 8, 1997.

Greene, Warner C. "AIDS and the Immune System." *Scientific American,* Sept. 1993.

Karl, Thomas R., Neville Nicholls, and Jonathan Gregory. "The Coming Climate." *Scientific American,* May 1997.

Leland, John, and Gregory Beals. "In Living Colors." *Newsweek,* May 5, 1997.

Lemann, Nicholas. "How the Seventies Changed America." *American Heritage,* July/Aug. 1991.

Life: The 100 Events That Shaped America, 1975.

Life: The 100 Most Important Americans of the Century, Fall 1990.

Low, Frances. ""A Chase Up into the Sky."" *American Heritage,* Oct. 1968.

McArthur, Benjamin. "The New Creationists." *American Heritage.* Nov. 1994.

Maule, Tex. "Bread-and-Butter Packers." *Sports Illustrated,* Jan. 23, 1967.

Novak, Robert D. "Betrayal at Yalta." *Washington Post,* Aug. 18, 1997.

"Pentagon Papers: The Secret War." *Time,* June 28, 1971.

"Protest, Detention, and Death under South Africa's State of Emergency." *Time,* Aug. 5, 1985.

"Red Moon over the U.S." *Time,* Oct. 14, 1957.

Riordan, Michael, and Lillian Hoddeson. "Birth of an Era." *Scientific American: Special Issue,* 1997.

Rosellini, Lynn. "Our Century." *U.S. News & World Report,* Aug. 28-Sept. 4, 1995.

Russell, George. "Going After the Crooks." *Time,* Dec. 1, 1986.

Sagan, Carl. "Science and Technology in the 20th Century." *New Perspectives Quarterly,* Summer 1996.

Seabrook, John. "Why Is the Force Still With Us?" *New Yorker,* Jan. 6, 1997.

Sears, Stephen W. " 'Shut the Goddam Plant!' " *American Heritage,* April/May 1982.

"The Sputnik." *Time,* Oct. 14, 1957.

Star, Alexander. "Don't Look Back." *New Yorker,* Feb. 3, 1997.

"*Star Wars:* The Year's Best Movie." *Time,* May 30, 1977.

Teale, Edwin. "Greatest Crime-Detection Laboratory Aids in Nation-Wide Man Hunts." *Popular Science,* Sept. 1935.

Teich, Mikuláš. "The 20th-Century Scientific-Technical Revolution." *History Today,* Nov. 1996.

" 'To All on Equal Terms.' " *Time,* May 24, 1954.

Weingroff, Richard F. "Three States Claim First Interstate Highway." *Public Roads,* June 1996.

INDEX

31, *110-111*, 183; and Cuban missile crisis, *130-131;* and INF Treaty, *170*

Nude Descending a Staircase (Duchamps), 52, *53*

O

O'Connor, Sandra Day, 145
Oil embargo, *158*
Old Faithful (geyser), *32*
Oliver, King (jazz musician), 73
O'Neill, Eugene, 50
Onizuka, Ellison S., *168*
OPEC, 158
Oswald, Lee Harvey, 134-136, *135*
"Over There" (Cohan), 60

P

Palestine, U.S. relations with, *31*
Panama Canal, 28
Pathfinder (Mars lander), *184-185*
Patricia (ship), *47*
Patton, George, 104; quoted, 105
Pearl Harbor, attack on, 31, *98-99*, 100-101
Pentagon Papers, 153
People's Republic of China. *See* China
Pershing II missiles, *170*
Piggly Wiggly grocery store, *57*
Pittsburgh Pirates, *40-41*
Plessy v. Ferguson, 34
Poland, and WWII, *96-97*, 105
Polio vaccine, *121*
Politics: Democratic National Convention (1968), *149;* isolationism, 30-31; presidential debates, *128;* radio broadcasts, 72. *See also specific organizations and persons*
Powell, Colin, *177;* quoted, 177
Presley, Elvis, *125*
Princip, Gavrilo, 56
Progressive movement, 31-32
Prohibition movement, 31, *67-69*
Psychoanalysis, 50
Public Works Administration, 86
Puerto Rico, and Spanish-American War, 30
Purvis, Melvin H., *90*

R

Rabin, Yitzhak, *31*
Radio: Atwater Kent breadboard, *72;* commercial radio, 30, 72; competition of with TV, 120; Scopes trial broadcast, *74-75*
Randolph, A. Philip, 132
Ray, James Earl, 148
Reagan, Ronald, *163;* and federal power, 32; and Iran hostage crisis, 165; quoted, 163, 168; and Soviet-U.S. relations, 6, 163, 170
Religion: and civil rights, 34, 35; Scopes trial, *74-75*
Republic Steel, employee rally (1937), 92, *93*
Resnik, Judith A., *168*
Robinson, Jackie, *112-113;* quoted, 113
Rock and roll music, *125*, 138
Roe v. Wade, 34, 154
Rogers, Will, quoted, 86

Rolling Stones, the (singing group), 138
Roosevelt, Eleanor, quoted, 100-101
Roosevelt, Franklin Delano: death of, 110; election of, 82; and Great Plains drought, 88; and New Deal, 32, 86, 92, 163; quoted, 82; with supporters, *87;* and WWII, *100;* at Yalta Conference, *105*
Roosevelt, Theodore, 28, 29, 31; quoted, 28, 32
Ruby, Jack, *135*, 136
Russia, and WWI, 60, 62. *See also* Soviet Union
Rustin, Bayard, 132
Ruth, Babe, *66;* quoted, 66

S

Sadat, Anwar el-, *162*
St. Louis World's Fair (1904), 44
Salk, Jonas, 121
San Francisco, California, earthquake (1906), *44-45*
Satellites, *127*, 129, 180
Saudi Arabia, and Gulf War, 174, 176
Saunders, Clarence, 57
Schneider, Ralph, 117
School integration. *See* Civil rights
Schwarzkopf, Norman H., *177*
Science. *See* Medical developments
Scobee, Francis R., *168*
Scopes, John, *74-75*
Segregation. *See* Civil rights
Selma, Alabama, and Freedom March, *142-143*
Selznick, David O., 95
Sexual Behavior in the Human Female (Kinsey), *115*
Sexual Behavior in the Human Male (Kinsey), *115*
Shaw, Bernard, quoted, 174
Shelley, Mary, 183
Shepard, Alan, Jr., 129
Silent Spring (Carson), *130*, 131
Sinclair, Upton, quoted, 45
Sirhan, Sirhan, 149
Smith, Howard, 139
Smith, Michael J., *168*
Smoking, warnings about, *143*
Social Security Act, 92
Sojourner (robot), 30, *184-185*
South Africa, *182*
Soviet Union: and Berlin airlift, 116; and Berlin Wall, 128, 172; collapse of, 31; and Cuban missile crisis, 130-131; and Korean War, 118; and Reagan era, 6, 163, 170; satellites launched by, *127*, 129; and WWII, 31, 105, 116
Space age, *6-7;* first man on Moon, 6, 30, *150*, 151, 168; first man to orbit Earth, 29, *129;* Hubble Space Telescope, *180-181;* Mars landing, 30, *184-185;* satellites, *127*, 129, 180; space shuttles, *168-169*, 180; spacewalk, *26-27*
Spanish-American War, 28, 30-31
Spirit of St. Louis (airplane), *76*, 77
Spock, Benjamin, 114
Sports: baseball, *20-21*, *40-41*, *66*, *112-113;* football, 144, *145;* golf, 35

Sputnik satellites, *127*, 129
Stalin, Joseph, 97, *105*, 116
Starr, Bart, *145*
Star Wars (movie), *161*
Steamboat Willie (cartoon), *78*
Steel industry, 39
Stimson, Henry, quoted, 100
Stock market: crash (1929), *78-79*, 81; securities fraud case (1990), *173*
Strikes, labor, 92, *93*
Students for a Democratic Society, 130, 139; quoted, 140
Suburban life, 33, *114-115*, 124
Suicide, assisted, *172*
Sullivan, Ed, *120*, 125
Super Bowl, 144, *145*
Supreme Court: and abortion, 34, 154; and birth control, 127, and civil rights, 34, 35, *122-123*, 126, 145
Surgeon general's report (1964), 143

T

Taft, William Howard, quoted, 68
Tax, income, enactment of, 32
Technology. *See* Business and industry; *specific products*
Television: competition of with other entertainment, 120; and Gulf War, 174, *176;* introduction of, 30; popular shows, *120-121;* presidential debates on, *128;* sports on, 144
Tennessee Valley Authority, 86
Tet offensive, *146*, 147
Three Mile Island accident, *162*
Thriller (record album), *167*
Tiananmen Square, *171*
Time magazine, quoted, 117, 170, 178, 180
Toast of the Town (TV show), *120*
Topeka, Kansas, school integration, *122-123*, 145
Toys, *Star Wars* memorabilia, *161*
Transistors, 30
Triangle Shirtwaist Factory fire, *50-51*
Truman, Harry S.: and armed forces integration, 35; and atomic bomb, 110; and Korean War, 118

U

United Auto Workers, 92
United Nations, 118, 174, 183
UNIVAC computer, 112
University of California at Berkeley, 139
U.S. Steel, 39
U.S.S.R. *See* Soviet Union

V

Vecchio, Mary Ann, *152-153*
Vietnam Veterans Memorial, *166-167*
Vietnam War: and Democratic National Convention (1968), 149; end of, 155; escalation of, *140-141;* and Kent State protests, *152-153;* and Pentagon Papers, 153; POW releases, *155;* soldiers killed and wounded in, *24-25;* and student activists, 139, 140, 149, *152-153;* Tet offensive, *146*, 147
Volstead Act, 68
Voting Rights Act, 142

W

Wagner Act of 1935, 92
Warren, Earl, *122-123;* quoted, 122, 123
Washington, D.C.: march on, *132-133;* Vietnam Veterans Memorial, *166-167*
Washington, George, 30
Washington Post, 153
Watergate scandal, *156-157*, 158
Wells, H. G., 183
Werblin, Sonny, quoted, 144
Westinghouse, 72
Westmoreland, William, quoted, 147
Who, the (singing group), 138
Wilkins, Roger, quoted, 137
Wilkins, Roy, quoted, 122
Wilson, Edmund, quoted, 82
Wilson, Woodrow: and Prohibition, 68; quoted, 56, 60; and woman suffrage ,70; and WWI, 31, 60, 62, 65
Women: and abortion legalization, 154; and birth control, 127; and civil rights, *34*, 139; feminist movement, *131;* and Gulf War, *174;* suffrage movement, 67, *70-71;* on Supreme Court, 35; as workers, *16-17*, 34, 50, 64, 131. *See also specific persons*
Women's Christian Temperance Union, 67
Wong, H. S., 94
Woods, Tiger, 35
Woodstock Festival, *151*
World Series, *40-41*, 66
World's Fair (1904), 44
World War I: Belleau Wood battle, 64; casualties in, 63; and employment, 33; events leading to, 31, 56, 60; and immigration, 49; and Prohibition, 67; recruiting posters, 60, *63;* significance of, 29; Treaty of Versailles, 65; U.S. entry into, 60; U.S. supply train, *62-63;* victory medal, *64;* victory parade, *64-65*
World War II: armed forces integration after, 35; and baby boom, 114; Battle of the Bulge, *104-105;* Battle of Midway, 101; and Communist expansion, 105, 117, 118; and computers, 30, 112; and consumer economy, 33; D-Day invasion, *102-103;* and employment, *16-17*, 33, 34; events leading to, 31, 65, 96; Iwo Jima landing, *106-107*, 110; and Japanese invasion of China, 94; Pearl Harbor attack, *98-99*, 100-101; suburban growth after, 33; U.S. internment camps, 34, *100-101;* women workers during, *16-17*, 34; Yalta Conference, *105*, 116
World Wide Web, 178
Wright, Orville, 6, 30, *42-43*
Wright, Wilbur, 6, 30, *42-43*

Y

Yalta Conference, *105*, 116
Yellowstone National Park, *32*
Young, Cy, 40

Z

Zapruder, Abraham, film by, 134, *135*
Ziegler, Ronald L., quoted, 156

TIME LIFE BOOKS

Time-Life Books is a division of Time Life Inc.

TIME LIFE INC.
PRESIDENT and CEO: George Artandi

TIME-LIFE BOOKS
PRESIDENT: Stephen R. Frary
PUBLISHER/MANAGING EDITOR: Neil Kagan

OUR AMERICAN CENTURY
Events That Shaped the Century

EDITORS: Sarah Brash, Loretta Britten
DIRECTOR, NEW PRODUCT DEVELOPMENT:
Elizabeth D. Ward
MARKETING DIRECTORS: Joseph A. Kuna, Pamela R. Farrell

Deputy Editors: Mary Mayberry (principal), Charles J. Hagner
Marketing Manager: Janine Wilkin
Associate Editors/Research and Writing: Nancy C. Blodgett,
Stephanie Summers Henke
Picture Associate: Anne Whittle
Senior Copyeditor: Anne Farr
Technical Art Specialist: John Drummond
Picture Coordinator: Betty H. Weatherley
Editorial Assistant: Christine Higgins

Design for **Our American Century** by Antonio Alcalá,
Studio A, Alexandria, Virginia.

Special Contributors: Laura Foreman, Glen B. Ruh, Robert
Speziale, Jim Watson (editing); Ronald H. Bailey, Maggie
Debelius (writing); Rachel Barenbaum, Mary Jo Binker,
Marilyn Murphy Terrell (research/writing); Ann-Louise G.
Gates, Mimi Harrison, Mary Suro (research); Marti Davila,
Richard Friend, Christina Hagopian, Henry Quiroga (design);
Susan Nedrow (index).

Correspondents: Maria Vincenza Aloisi (Paris), Christine Hinze
(London), Christina Lieberman (New York). Valuable assistance
was also provided by Angelika Lemmer (Bonn) and Bogdan
Turek (Warsaw).

Director of Finance: Christopher Hearing
Directors of Book Production: Marjann Caldwell, Patricia Pascale
Director of Publishing Technology: Betsi McGrath
Director of Photography and Research: John Conrad Weiser
Director of Editorial Administration: Barbara Levitt
Production Manager: Gertraude Schaefer
Quality Assurance Manager: James King
Chief Librarian: Louise D. Forstall

EDITORIAL CONSULTANT
Richard B. Stolley is currently senior editorial adviser at Time
Inc. After 19 years at *Life* magazine as a reporter, bureau chief,
and assistant managing editor he became the first managing
editor of *People* magazine, a position he held with great success
for eight years. He then returned to *Life* magazine as managing
editor and later served as editorial director for all Time Inc.
magazines. In 1997 Stolley received the Henry Johnson Fisher
Award for Lifetime Achievement, the magazine industry's highest honor.

Other History Publications:

What Life Was Like
The American Story
Voices of the Civil War
The American Indians
Lost Civilizations
Mysteries of the Unknown
Time Frame
The Civil War
Cultural Atlas

Library of Congress Cataloging-in-Publication Data
Events that shaped the century / by the editors of Time-Life
Books, Alexandria, Virginia ; with a foreword by Buzz Aldrin.
p. cm.—(Our American century)
Includes bibliographical references and index.
ISBN 0-7835-5502-4
ISBN Trade Edition 0-7370-0200-X
1. United States—History—20th century—Chronology.
2. United States—Social life and customs—20th century.
I. Time-Life Books.   II. Series.
E741.E94 1998
973.9'02'02—dc21   97-53235
                                    CIP

For information on and a full description of any of the Time-
Life Books series listed above, please call 1-800-621-7026 or
write:

Reader Information
Time-Life Customer Service
P.O. Box C-32068
Richmond, Virginia 23261-2068